GRADE

Mathematics

Intervention Activities

Table of Contents

Using Mathematics Intervention Activities

Current research indicates that literacy activities that engage students in familiar, real-world math situations are essential for math skill development. The Mathematics Intervention Activities series offers activities that are carefully crafted to help students grow in language and literacy while acquiring core grade-level math content.

Effective mathematics activities provide students with opportunities to:

- Strengthen the language and literacy skills needed to develop math proficiency

- Relate math concepts to real-life situations

- Develop math computation and application skills

Although some students master these skills easily during regular classroom instruction, many others need additional reteaching opportunities to master these essential skills. The Mathematics Intervention Activities series provides easy-to-use, five-day intervention units for Grades K–5. These units are structured around a research-based model-guide-practice-apply approach. You can use these activities in a variety of intervention models, including Response to Intervention (RTI).

Standards-Based Mathematics Awareness Skills in Intervention Activities

The mathematics strategies found in the Intervention Activities series are introduced developmentally and spiral from one grade to the next. The chart below shows the types of skill areas addressed at each grade level in this series.

Mathematics Intervention Activities Series Words	K	1	2	3	4	5
Counting & Cardinality	✔					
Number & Operations	✔	✔	✔	✔	✔	✔
Algebraic Thinking	✔	✔	✔	✔	✔	✔
Fractions				✔	✔	✔
Measurement & Data	✔	✔	✔	✔	✔	✔
Geometry	✔	✔	✔	✔	✔	✔

Getting Started

In just five simple steps, Mathematics Intervention Activities provides everything you need to identify students' needs and to provide targeted intervention.

1. PRE-ASSESS to identify students'
mathematics needs. Use the pre-assessment to identify the skills your students need to master.

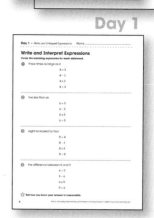

2. MODEL the skill.
Every five-day unit targets a specific mathematics area. On Day 1, use the teacher prompts and reproducible activity page to introduce and model the skill.

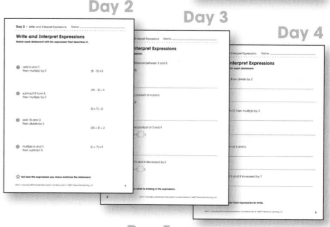

Day 1

3. GUIDE, PRACTICE, and APPLY.
Use the reproducible practice activities for Days 2, 3, and 4 to build students' understanding and skill proficiency.

Day 2

Day 3

Day 4

4. MONITOR progress.
Administer the Day 5 reproducible assessment to monitor each student's progress and to make instructional decisions.

Day 5

5. POST-ASSESS to document student progress.
Use the post-assessment to measure students' progress as a result of your interventions.

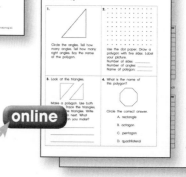

Using Intervention for RTI

According to the National Center on Response to Intervention, RTI "integrates assessment and intervention within a multi-level prevention system to maximize student achievement and to reduce behavior problems." This model of instruction and assessment allows schools to identify at-risk students, monitor their progress, provide research-proven interventions, and "adjust the intensity and nature of those interventions depending on a student's responsiveness."

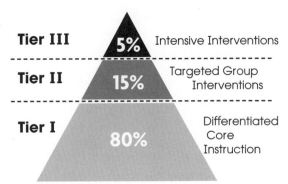

RTI models vary from district to district, but the most prevalent model is a three-tiered approach to instruction and assessment.

The Three Tiers of RTI	Using Intervention Activities
Tier I: Differentiated Core Instruction • Designed for all students • Preventive, proactive, standards-aligned instruction • Whole- and small-group differentiated instruction • Ninety-minute, daily core reading instruction in the five essential skill areas: Mathematics, phonemic awareness, comprehension, vocabulary, fluency	• Use whole-group mathematics mini-lessons to introduce and guide practice with mathematics strategies that all students need to learn. • Use any or all of the units in the order that supports your core instructional program.
Tier II: Targeted Group Interventions • For at-risk students • Provide thirty minutes of daily instruction beyond the ninety-minute Tier I core instruction • Instruction is conducted in small groups of three to five students with similar needs	• Select units based on your students' areas of need (the pre-assessment can help you identify these). • Use the units as week-long, small-group mini-lessons.
Tier III: Intensive Interventions • For high-risk students experiencing considerable difficulty • Provide up to sixty minutes of additional intensive intervention each day in addition to the ninety-minute Tier I core instruction • More intense and explicit instruction • Instruction conducted individually or with smaller groups of one to three students with similar needs	• Select units based on your students' areas of need. • Use the units as one component of an intensive mathematics intervention program.

Mathematics Intervention Activities Grade 5 • ©2014 Newmark Learning, LLC

Overview   Order of Operations

Directions and Sample Answers for Activity Pages

Day 1	See "Model the Skill" below.
Day 2	Read the directions aloud. Review the order of the steps in evaluating an expression. Point out that the expressions on this page are similar to those on the previous activity page, but parentheses have been added. Remind students to evaluate the expression within the parentheses first before conducting any other operation. Students should note that finding the difference within the parentheses first changes the factors and the final solution. (**1.** 5 x 2 = 10; **2.** 24 ÷ 4 = 6; **3.** 32 ÷ 4 = 8; **4.** 7 x 6 = 42)
Day 3	Read the directions aloud. Point out that the column on the left shows four expressions and the column on the right shows four solutions. Remind students to evaluate the expression within the parentheses first. (**1.** 12; **2.** 7; **3.** 15; **4.** 1)
Day 4	Read the directions aloud. Point out that each expression consists of two sets of parentheses. Guide students to evaluate the expressions within both parentheses before performing the operation indicated between the sets of parentheses. (**1.** 4 x 6 = 24; **2.** 24 + 14 = 38; **3.** 20 – 12 = 8; **4.** 0)
Day 5	Read the directions aloud. Observe as students complete the page. Do students evaluate the expressions within the parentheses first? Do they write the sub-step for their evaluation accurately? Use your observations to plan further instruction and review. (**1.** 6 – 2 = 4; **2.** 6 x 1 = 6; **3.** 48 ÷ 6 = 8; **4.** 15 – 7 = 8)

Model the Skill

◆ Hand out the Day 1 activity page.

◆ Write the equation 6 – 4 = 2 on the board. **Say:** *This is an equation. It uses numbers and symbols and an equal sign.* Write the expression 6 – 4 on the board. **Say:** *This is an expression. How is this different from the equation?* (It does not have an equal sign or a sum.) *Today, we will be evaluating expressions. When you evaluate an expression, you find the solution.*

◆ **Ask:** *What do you notice about the expression in problem 1?* (Possible answer: It has three numbers and two different operation symbols.) *To evaluate this expression, you complete the operations from left to right just as you read words in a sentence. What is 5 times 6?* (30) Point out where the product 30 is written as the first step in evaluating the expression. **Say:** *Now you can subtract 4 to finish evaluating the expression. What is 30 minus 4?* (26)

◆ Help students complete the activity page by evaluating the first part of each expression, recording the sub-step, and then finding the final solution. Students should note that, in problem 4, they should first find the product of 7 and 9 before subtracting 3. (**2.** 8 + 1 = 9; **3.** 4 – 4 = 0; **4.** 60)

Use Manipulatives

Use a set of cards numbered 0–9 as well as + and x symbol cards. Have students choose three number cards to generate an expression in the *a* x *b* + *c* format. Have them evaluate the expression. Then use pipe cleaners to form parentheses around the *b* + *c* portion of the expression. Have students evaluate this expression and compare solutions.

Order of Operations

Use the order of operations. Evaluate each expression.

 1

$$5 \times 6 \quad - \quad 4$$
$$\downarrow \qquad\qquad \downarrow$$

$$30 \quad - \quad 4 \quad = \quad \rule{3cm}{0.4pt}$$

 2

$$24 \div 3 \quad + \quad 1$$
$$\downarrow \qquad\qquad \downarrow$$

$$\rule{3cm}{0.4pt} \quad + \quad 1 \quad = \quad \rule{3cm}{0.4pt}$$

 3

$$32 \div 8 \quad - \quad 4$$
$$\downarrow \qquad\qquad \downarrow$$

$$\rule{2.5cm}{0.4pt} \; - \rule{2.5cm}{0.4pt} \; = \; \rule{2.5cm}{0.4pt}$$

 4

$$7 \times 9 - 3 = \rule{3cm}{0.4pt}$$

☆ **Tell what you did first to solve the problem.**

Order of Operations

Use the order of operations. Evaluate each expression.

$$5 \times (6 - 4)$$
$$\downarrow \qquad \downarrow$$

$$5 \times \underline{\qquad} \qquad = \qquad \underline{\qquad}$$

$$24 \qquad \div \qquad (3 + 1)$$
$$\downarrow \qquad\qquad \downarrow$$

$$\underline{\qquad} \div \underline{\qquad} = \underline{\qquad}$$

$$32 \qquad\qquad \div \qquad (8 - 4)$$
$$\downarrow \qquad\qquad\qquad \downarrow$$

$$\underline{\qquad} \bigcirc \underline{\qquad} = \underline{\qquad}$$

$$7 \times (9 - 3) = \underline{\qquad}$$

⭐ **Tell how evaluating an expression with parentheses affects the solution.**

Order of Operations

Draw a line to match the expression to the correct evaluation.

①   2 x (9 – 3)   15

②   28 ÷ (7 – 3)   1

③   3 + (4 x 3)   12

④   (24 – 16) ÷ 8   7

☆ **Tell how you evaluate an expression with parentheses.**

Order of Operations

Use the order of operations. Evaluate each expression.

 1

$(2 \times 2) \quad \times \quad (3 + 3)$
   ↓   ↓

_____ X _____ = _____

 2

$(25 - 1) \quad + \quad (7 \times 2)$
   ↓   ↓

_____ + _____ = _____

 3

$(4 \times 5) \quad - \quad (6 \times 2)$
   ↓   ↓

_____ ◯ _____ = _____

4

$(2 \times 8) - (9 + 7) =$ _____

★ **Tell how you solved the problem.**

Assessment

Use the order of operations. Evaluate each expression.

48   ÷   8 – 2

_____ ◯ _____ = _____

(4 + 2)   x   6 – 5)

_____ ◯ _____ = _____

48   ÷   (8 – 2)

_____ ◯ _____ = _____

(3 x 5) – (49 ÷ 7) = _____

☆ **Tell about the order in which you evaluated the expression.**

Overview Write and Interpret Expressions

Directions and Sample Answers for Activity Pages

Day 1	See "Model the Skill" below.
Day 2	Read the directions aloud. Review with students the symbols used for each of the four operations. Point out that not every expression will be used. Guide students to write the expression that matches each statement. Remind them that they do not need to find a solution for the expression. (**1.** (6 + 7) x 3; **2.** (8 – 5) x 5; **3.** (15 + 3) ÷ 2; **4.** (6 x 7) – 5)
Day 3	Read the directions aloud. Point out that portions of each expression are given and that students need to write in the missing portions. Guide students to see that the symbols are missing in problems 1 and 2 while the numbers are missing in problems 3 and 4. Remind students to look at the language of each statement to help them determine the symbols and the placement of the numbers. (**1.** 9 x (5 – 3); **2.** (4 x 6) – 8; **3.** (2 x 4) + 7 or (4 x 2) + 7; **4.** (3 x 4) – 6 or (4 x 3) – 6)
Day 4	Read the directions aloud. Point out that students must write the entire expression for each problem on this activity page. Remind students to use the language of each statement to help them determine which operation symbols to use. (**1.** (12 + 8) ÷ 2 or (8 + 12) ÷ 2; **2.** (17 – 9) x 3; **3.** 5 x (4 + 6), 5 x (6 + 4), (4 + 6) x 5, or (6 + 4) x 5; **4.** (6 x 8) + 7 or (8 x 6) + 7)
Day 5	Read the directions aloud. Point out that the directions for problems 1 and 2 are different than the directions for problems 3 and 4. Observe as students complete the page. Do students match the correct operation symbols to the language used in the statement? Do they write an expression that matches the statement? Use your observations to plan further instruction and review. (**1.** 9 – 4; **2.** (8 x 6) + 5; **3.** (9 x 4) ÷ 3 or (4 x 9) ÷ 3; **4.** 2 x (10 – 7) or (10 – 7) x 2)

Model the Skill

◆ Hand out the Day 1 activity page.

◆ Write the equation 6 + 7 = 13 on the board. **Say:** *This is an equation. It uses numbers and symbols and an equal sign.* Write the expression 6 + 7 on the board. **Ask:** *How is this different from the equation?* (It does not have an equal sign or a sum.) **Say:** *This is an expression. An expression is similar to an equation in that it uses numbers and symbols, but it does not include an equal sign or an answer. We will be writing expressions but not solving the problems.*

◆ Read aloud the directions on the activity page. **Say:** *Think about the statement "three times as large as." Does that wording indicate that the values should be added or subtracted?* (no) Guide students to see that the values need to be multiplied. Allow them to use counters or draw a picture to see the operation. **Say:** *Find the expression that matches the statement.* (4 x 3)

◆ Help students complete the activity page, focusing on the language structure of each statement and its corresponding expression. Discuss what other phrases might be used to indicate each operation. (**2.** 6 – 5; **3.** 8 + 4; **4.** 9 – 6)

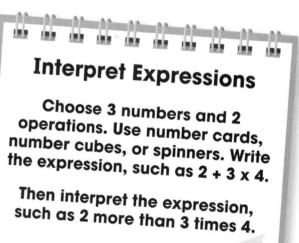

Interpret Expressions

Choose 3 numbers and 2 operations. Use number cards, number cubes, or spinners. Write the expression, such as 2 + 3 x 4.

Then interpret the expression, such as 2 more than 3 times 4.

Write and Interpret Expressions

Circle the matching expression for each statement.

1   three times as large as 4

$$4 + 3$$
$$4 - 3$$
$$4 \times 3$$
$$4 \div 3$$

2   five less than six

$$6 + 5$$
$$6 - 5$$
$$6 \times 5$$
$$6 \div 5$$

3   eight increased by four

$$8 + 4$$
$$8 - 4$$
$$8 \times 4$$
$$8 \div 4$$

4   the difference between 6 and 9

$$6 + 9$$
$$9 - 6$$
$$6 \times 9$$
$$9 \div 6$$

☆ **Tell how you know your answer is reasonable.**

Write and Interpret Expressions

Match each statement with the expression that describes it.

1 add 6 and 7,
   then multiply by 3 $(8 - 5) \times 5$

2 subtract 5 from 8,
   then multiply by 5 $(6 \times 7w) - 5$

3 add 15 and 3,
   then divide by 2 $(15 + 3) \div 2$

4 multiply 6 and 7,
   then subtract 5 $(6 + 7) \times 3$

☆ **Tell how the expression you chose matches the statement.**

Write and Interpret Expressions

Complete each expression.

1 9 times the difference between 3 and 5

9 ◯ (5 ◯ 3)

---

2 8 less than the product of 4 and 6

(4 ◯ 6) ◯ 8

---

3 7 more than the product of 2 and 4

(☐ x ☐) + (☐)

---

4 the product of 3 and 4 decreased by 6

(☐ x ☐) – (☐)

☆ **Tell how you know what is missing in the expression.**

Write and Interpret Expressions

Write an expression for each statement.

1 add 12 and 8, then divide by 2

_____

_____

2 subtract 9 from 17, then multiply by 3

_____

_____

3 5 times the sum of 4 and 6

_____

_____

4 the product of 6 and 8 increased by 7

_____

☆ **Tell how you know what expression to write.**

Assessment

Circle the matching expression for each statement.

1 nine decreased by 4

 9 + 4

 9 – 4

 9 x 4

 9 ÷ 4

2 five more than the product of eight and six

 5 + (8 + 6)

 (8 x 6) + 5

 (8 ÷ 6) – 5

Write an expression for each statement.

3 multiply 9 and 4, then divide by 3

_____

4 2 times the difference between 7 and 10

_____

☆ **Tell how you solved the problem.**

Overview Patterns and Ordered Pairs

Directions and Sample Answers for Activity Pages

Day 1	See "Model the Skill" below.
Day 2	Read the directions aloud. Point out that the rule for each pattern is given. Then guide students to see that the table for the ordered pairs is a vertical format of the horizontal table with the terms from the top pattern being the *x* values and the terms from the bottom pattern being the *y* values. Students should note that the *y* value is 5 times the *x* value in problem 3. (**1.** 8, 10; **2.** 18, 16; 9, 8; **3.** 4, 5; 20, 25)
Day 3	Read the directions aloud. Point out that the patterns are all in the vertical format and the rules for the *x* and *y* values are given. After students complete the tables, they will record the ordered pairs using the parentheses format shown below each table. Students should note that the *x* value in any ordered pair is written before the *y* value. (**1.** 9, 12; (2, 6), (3, 9), (4, 12); **2.** 16; 6, 8; (4, 2), (8, 4), (12, 6), (16, 8); **3.** 2, 1; 9, 6, 3; (4, 12), (3, 9), (2, 6), (1, 3))
Day 4	Read the directions aloud. Point out that the patterns are given, but the rules are not. Guide students to look for the relationship between the *x* and *y* values and then write the rules for both the *x* values and the *y* values. To find the rules for the *x* and *y* values, students should look at the relationship between the adjacent numbers in each column. (**1.** *y* is double the value of *x*; *x* is add 3 and *y* is add 6; **2.** *y* is double the value of *x*; *x* is subtract 2 and *y* is subtract 4; **3.** *y* is 4 times *x*; *x* is add 1 and *y* is add 4; **4.** *y* is *x* divided by 3; *x* is subtract 3 and *y* is subtract 1)
Day 5	Read the directions aloud. Observe as students complete the page. Do students follow the given pattern rule? Do they look at how the *y* value compares to the *x* value to determine the relationship between the values of the ordered pair? Use your observations to plan further instruction and review. (**1.** 10, 5; 3, 2, 1; **2.** 6, 8; 18, 24; **3.** *y* is 2 times *x*; *x* is add 2 and *y* is add 4; **4.** *y* is *x* divided by 6; *x* is subtract 6 and *y* is subtract 1)

Model the Skill

◆ Hand out the Day 1 activity page. Direct students to the first problem. **Say:** *We are going to extend number patterns. The rule is given. If you add 3 to 3, is the sum 6?* (yes) *If you add 3 to 6, is the sum 9?* (yes) *What is the sum of 9 and 3?* (12) *If you continue the pattern, what is the last number in the pattern?* (15) Have students look at the second sequence of numbers in problem 1, noting that each subsequent term is 6 more than the previous term. Guide students to extend the pattern. (24, 30)

◆ **Ask:** *How are the rules for problem 2 different from the rules for problem 1?* (They are subtraction instead of addition.) Guide students to see how each number in the pattern follows the given rule. **Ask:** *How do you find the next two numbers in the top pattern?* (Subtract 2 from 6 to get 4. Then subtract 2 from 4 to get 2.) *How can you continue the bottom pattern?* (Subtract 4 from 12 for a difference of 8. Then subtract 4 from 8 for a difference of 4.)

◆ Help students complete the activity page by following the given rule to continue each pattern. Students should note that the number in the second pattern for problem 4 is half of the number in the first pattern. (**3.** 4, 5; 16, 20; **4.** 28, 32, 36; 14, 16, 18)

Use Manipulatives

Have pairs of students drop a counter on a hundreds chart.

If the number is low, have students create a pattern of adding 2, 3, 4, or 5.

If the number is high, have students create a pattern of subtracting 5, 4, 3, or 2.

Patterns and Ordered Pairs

Follow the rule to complete each pattern.

  1

add 3	3	6	9		

add 6	6	12	18		

2

subtract 2	10	8	6		

subtract 4	20	16	12		

3

add 1	1	2	3		

add 4	4	8	12		

4

add 4	20	24			

add 2	10	0			

☆ **Tell how the patterns are related.**

Patterns and Ordered Pairs

Complete each pattern. Then write the ordered pairs in the table.

add 1	1	2	3	4	5
add 2	2	4	6		

x	y
1	2
2	4
3	6
4	
5	

subtract 2	24	22	20		
subtract 1	12	11	10		

x	y
24	12
22	11
20	

add 1	1	2	3		
add 5	5	10	15		

x	y
1	
2	
3	

⭐ **Tell about the relationship of the ordered pairs.**

Patterns and Ordered Pairs

Follow the rules to find the missing values. Then write the ordered pairs.

x add 1	y add 3
1	3
2	6
3	
4	

(1, 3), (2, ____), (3, ____), (____ , ____)

x add 4	y add 2
4	2
8	4
12	

(4, ____), (8, ____), (____ , ____), (____ , ____)

x subtract 1	y subtract 3
4	12
3	

(____ , ____), (____ , ____), (____ , ____), (____ , ____)

☆ **Tell how you know which numbers to write in the ordered pair.**

Patterns and Ordered Pairs

Look for a relationship in the ordered pairs. Then write the rules.

1

x	y
3	6
6	12
9	18
12	24

Relationship: _____

Rules: _____

_____

2

x	y
10	20
8	16
6	12
4	8

Relationship: _____

Rules: _____

_____

3

x	y
1	4
2	8
3	12
4	16

Relationship: _____

Rules: _____

_____

4

x	y
21	7
18	6
15	5
12	4

Relationship: _____

Rules: _____

_____

⭐ **Tell how you determined the rules.**

Assessment

Complete each pattern.

Subtract 5	25	20	15		

Subtract 1	5	4			

2

Add 2	Add 6
2	6
4	12

Look for a relationship in the ordered pairs. Then write the rules.

3

x	y
10	20
12	24
14	28
16	32

Relationship: _____

Rules: _____

_____

4

x	y
30	5
24	4
18	3
12	2

Relationship: _____

Rules: _____

_____

☆ **Tell how you know the relationship between the pair.**

Overview   Decimal Place Value

Directions and Sample Answers for Activity Pages

Day 1	See "Model the Skill" below.
Day 2	Read the directions aloud. Point out that the numbers are given in a place-value chart for problems 1 and 2 but not for problems 3 and 4. Encourage students to read each number slowly as they write the corresponding words. Remind students that the word **and** is used to indicate the switch between the whole number portion and the decimal portion of a number. (**1.** five hundred twenty-three and four-tenths; **2.** seventy and eight hundred ninety-one thousandths; **3.** four and fifty-six hundredths; **4.** three hundred twenty-one and sixty-five thousandths)
Day 3	Read the directions aloud. Remind students that the digits to the right of the decimal point should be expressed as fractions. Point out that zeros are not represented in the expanded form. (**1.** 70 + 4 + 2/10 + 1/100; **2.** 8 + 9/100 + 6/1,000; **3.** 300 + 50 + 1/10 + 8/100; **4.** 200 + 6 + 4/100 + 7/1,000)
Day 4	Read the directions aloud. Encourage students to think of the standard form of each expanded form or word form to guide their thinking. (**1.** 7 + 5 + 9/10; **2.** eight hundred four; **3.** 36.2000; **4.** 100 + 70 + 70/10 + 5/1,000)
Day 5	Read the directions aloud. Observe as students complete the page. Do students write the correct missing form? Do they represent only the nonzero digits in the expanded and word forms? Use your observations to plan further instruction and review. (**1.** 6 + 1/10 + 7/100; **2.** 35.2; **3.** four and five hundred seventy-nine thousandths; **4.** 800 + 2 + 6/100)

Model the Skill

◆ Hand out the Day 1 activity page.

◆ **Say:** *Look at the place-value chart.* **Ask:** *How many places are shown on this chart?* (6) *Which place is the greatest?* (hundreds) Point out the decimal point and explain that three places are to the left of the decimal point and three places are to the right of the decimal point. **Ask:** *How does the tens place compare to the ones place?* (The tens place is 10 times more than the ones place.) Explain that each place is 1/10 of the place to its left—the tenths place is 1/10 of the ones place.

◆ Have a student read the number word in problem 1. Point out that **and** indicates there is a fraction of a number, or a decimal amount, that follows the whole number portion. **Ask:** *How do we write one hundred three in the place-value chart?* (1 in the hundreds, 0 in the tens, and 3 in the ones) Help students who might have difficulty see why a zero is needed in the tens place. **Ask:** *How do we write nine-tenths in the chart?* (9 in the tenths place) Demonstrate how to use the numbers written in the chart to write the standard form. (103.9) Have students look at the standard form and say the number aloud, making sure that it matches the word form.

◆ Help students complete the activity page. Remind them of the importance of zero in place value as they solve problems 2 and 4. (**2.** 40.567; **3.** 2.13; **4.** 89.003)

> ## Use Number Cards and a Place-Value Chart
> Use two sets of cards numbered 0–9 and a place-value chart that includes three decimal places. Draw between three and six cards. Display them in the place-value chart.
>
> Read the number and write it in both standard and expanded forms.

Decimal Place Value

Write each number. Use the place-value chart to help you.

hundreds	tens	ones	.	tenths	hundredths	thousandths
			.			

1 one hundred three and nine-tenths

_____

2 forty and five hundred sixty-seven thousandths

_____

3 two and thirteen-hundredths

_____

4 eighty-nine and three-thousandths

_____

☆ **Tell how place value helps you write a number.**

Decimal Place Value

Read each number. Write its word name. Use the place-value chart to help you.

 1

hundreds	tens	ones	.	tenths	hundredths	thousandths
5	2	3	.	4		

_____

2

hundreds	tens	ones	.	tenths	hundredths	thousandths
	7	0	.	8	9	1

_____

3

4.56

_____

4

321.065

_____

☆ **Tell how place value helps you read a number.**

Decimal Place Value

Write each number in expanded form. Use the place-value chart to help you.

hundreds	tens	ones	.	tenths	hundredths	thousandths
			.			

1 74.21

$$70 + 4 + \frac{2}{10} + \underline{\hspace{2cm}}$$

2 8.096

$$\underline{\hspace{2cm}} + \frac{9}{100} + \underline{\hspace{2cm}}$$

3 350.18

$$300 + \underline{\hspace{1.5cm}} + \underline{\hspace{1.5cm}} + \underline{\hspace{1.5cm}}$$

4 206.047

$$\underline{\hspace{1.5cm}} + \underline{\hspace{1.5cm}} + \underline{\hspace{1.5cm}} + \underline{\hspace{1.5cm}}$$

☆ **Tell how you know the value of each digit in a number.**

Decimal Place Value

Cross out the form that does not match.

 1

7.59	seven and fifty-nine hundredths
$7 + 5 + \frac{9}{10}$	$7 + \frac{5}{10} + \frac{9}{100}$

 2

eight hundred four	$8 + \frac{4}{100}$
8.04	eight and four-hundredths

 3

$30 + 6 + \frac{2}{1,000}$	36.002
thirty-six and two-thousandths	36.2000

4

one hundred seven and seven hundred five thousandths	$100 + 70 + \frac{70}{10} + \frac{5}{1,000}$
$100 + 7 + \frac{7}{10} + \frac{5}{1,000}$	107.705

⭐ **Tell how you know which number does not match.**

Assessment

Complete the chart to show each number in each form.

	Standard Form	Expanded Form	Word Form
1	6.17		six and seventeen-hundredths
2		$30 + 5 + \frac{2}{10}$	thirty-five and two-tenths
3	4.579	$4 + \frac{5}{10} + \frac{7}{100} + \frac{9}{1,000}$	
4	802.06		eight hundred two and six-hundredths

☆ **Tell how the last digit in a number compares to the digit to its left.**

    Unit 4 • Mathematics Intervention Activities Grade 5 • ©2014 Newmark Learning, LLC

Overview Powers of 10

Directions and Sample Answers for Activity Pages

Day 1	See "Model the Skill" below.
Day 2	Read the directions aloud. Point out that the problems involve decimals. Guide students to use the pattern in problem 1 to help them in solving the other problems. Remind them that the number of zeros in the factor of 10 indicates how many spaces to move the decimal point. Therefore, if a number is multiplied by 1,000, the decimal point should move three places to the right. (**1.** 2,100; **2.** 43, 430; **3.** 928; **4.** 56)
Day 3	Read the directions aloud. Point out that each problem involves dividing by a power of 10. Discuss that when dividing, the answer is less than the original value. Guide students to use the pattern shown in problem 1 to help solve the other problems. Students should see that when the divisor is 100, there are two fewer zeros in the quotient than in the dividend. (**1.** 97; **2.** 2,340; 234; **3.** 58; **4.** 6,010)
Day 4	Read the directions aloud. Point out that the problems on this page involve decimals. Guide students to see that the number of zeros in the divisor indicates the number of places the decimal point moves to the left in the quotient. Therefore, if a number is divided by 100, the decimal point should move two places to the left. (**1.** 0.5936; **2.** 0.0471, 0.00471; **3.** 0.0249; **4.** 0.09028)
Day 5	Read the directions aloud. Observe as students complete the page. Do students move the decimal point according to the number of zeros? Do they move the decimal right when multiplying and left when dividing? Use your observations to plan further instruction and review. (**1.** 5,060; **2.** 920; **3.** 847; **4.** 0.3215)

Model the Skill

◆ Hand out the Day 1 activity page.

◆ **Say:** *The first row of blocks shows the multiplication of 9 times 1 as there are 9 groups of 1. What multiplication does the second row of blocks show?* (9 times 10; 9 groups of 10) Lead students to look at each row of blocks and connect it to a multiplication equation in problem 1. **Ask:** *What pattern do you see in the equations?* (Possible answer: The product has the same number of zeros as the second factor.) *What is the product of 9 and 1,000?* (9,000)

◆ Guide students to use the pattern shown to find each product in problem 2. (1,500, 15,000) **Ask:** *If you multiply a whole number by 100, how many zeros will you add to the factor when writing the product?* (two) Point out that you are moving the decimal point one place to the right when multiplying by 10, two places to the right when multiplying by 100, and three places to the right when multiplying by 1,000.

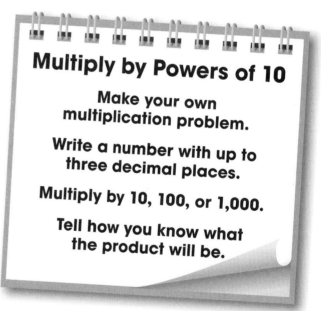

Multiply by Powers of 10

Make your own multiplication problem.

Write a number with up to three decimal places.

Multiply by 10, 100, or 1,000.

Tell how you know what the product will be.

◆ Help students complete the activity page by using the patterns that they discovered in problems 1 and 2 to solve problems 3 and 4. Students should note that the number of zeros in the factor of 10 indicates the number of zeros in the product. (**3.** 361,000; **4.** 4,800)

Powers of 10

Multiply. Use patterns to help you.

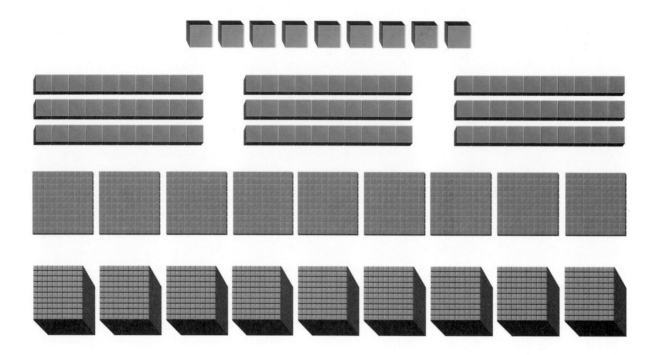

1. 9 x 10 = 90

   9 x 100 = 900

   9 x 1,000 = _____

2. 15 x 10 = 150

   15 x 100 = _____

   15 x 1,000 = _____

3. 361 x 1,000 = _____

4. 48 x 100 = _____

☆ **Tell how you know how many zeros there should be in a product.**

Powers of 10

Multiply. Use patterns to help you.

1 2.1 x 10 = 21

2.1 x 100 = 210

2.1 x 1,000 = _____

2 0.43 x 10 = 4.3

0.43 x 100 = _____

0.43 x 1,000 = _____

3 9.28 x 100 = _____

4 0.056 x 1,000 = _____

☆ **Tell how the placement of the decimal point changes when a decimal is multiplied by 1,000.**

Name _____

Powers of 10

Divide. Use patterns to help you.

1 $97{,}000 \div 10 = 9{,}700$

$97{,}000 \div 100 = 970$

$97{,}000 \div 1{,}000 =$ _____

2 $234{,}000 \div 10 = 23{,}400$

$234{,}000 \div 100 =$ _____

$234{,}000 \div 1{,}000 =$ _____

3 $58{,}000 \div 1{,}000 =$ _____

4 $601{,}000 \div 100 =$ _____

☆ **Tell about the pattern of zeros in the quotient when dividing by powers of 10.**

Powers of 10

Divide. Use patterns to help you.

1 593.6 ÷ 10 = 59.36

593.6 ÷ 100 = 5.936

593.6 ÷ 1,000 = _____

2 4.71 ÷ 10 = 0.471

4.71 ÷ 100 = _____

4.71 ÷ 1,000 = _____

3 24.9 ÷ 1,000 = _____

4 9.028 ÷ 100 = _____

☆ **Tell how the placement of the decimal point changes when a decimal is divided by 100.**

Assessment

Solve each problem. Use patterns to help you.

① 506 x 10 = _____

_____

② 0.92 x 1,000 = _____

_____

③ 847,000 ÷ 1,000 = _____

_____

④ 32.15 ÷ 100 = _____

☆ **Tell how you know which way to move the decimal point.**

Overview   Compare Decimals

Directions and Sample Answers for Activity Pages

Day 1	See "Model the Skill" below.
Day 2	Read the directions aloud. Point out the reference box that reminds students of the meaning of each symbol. Remind students to compare the digits beginning on the left and move right until they find differing digits. Then have students put their pencil point closest to the greater number and draw the symbol so that it points to the lesser number. (**1.** <; **2.** >; **3.** <; **4.** =)
Day 3	Read the directions aloud. Point out that all the numbers used in the comparisons are shown in the place-value chart. Guide students to see that the numbers have different numbers of digits. Tell students to add zeros to the right of a number so that both numbers have the same number of digits. For example, to compare the two numbers in problem 1, students should compare 8.92 and 8.90. Then they can clearly see which number is greater. (**1.** >; **2.** <; **3.** >; **4.** <)
Day 4	Read the directions aloud. Point out the reference box that reminds students of the meaning of each symbol. Guide students to see that the same numbers are used in the comparisons in problems 1 and 2. Encourage students to read each comparison after writing a symbol to check their work. (**1.** >, <; **2.** <, >; **3.** =; **4.** <)
Day 5	Read the directions aloud. Observe as students complete the page. Do students remember to compare the places starting on the left? Do they write the correct comparison symbols? Use your observations to plan further instruction and review. (**1.** >; **2.** <; **3.** =; **4.** >)

Model the Skill

◆ Hand out the Day 1 activity page.

◆ **Say:** *A place-value chart can help you compare decimal numbers. What are the numbers shown in the first place-value chart?* (0.4 and 0.6) *Both numbers have the same number of digits and the same number of decimal places. How do you compare these numbers?* (Possible answer: Start at the digit on the left and compare the digits in the same place. If the digits are the same, move to the next digit to the right. Then compare the two digits to see which is greater.) *Which number is greater?* (0.6) Have students circle that number in the chart. **Say:** *If 0.6 is greater than 0.4, then 0.4 is less than 0.6.*

◆ Direct students to the two statements next to the chart. **Ask:** *Which statement is correct?* (0.4 is less than 0.6.) Have students circle the correct statement. You may wish to have them cross out the incorrect statement.

◆ Direct students to problem 2. **Ask:** *Which place will you use to compare these two numbers?* (the hundredths place) Have students circle the digit in the hundredths place that is greater. Then guide them to circle the correct statement. (0.58 is less than 0.59.)

◆ Help students complete the activity page by comparing the digits from left to right and circling the greater digit. Then guide students to circle the correct statement next to each chart. (**3.** 0.073 is greater than 0.013. **4.** 0.512 is greater than 0.312.)

Comparing Game

Give each student a set of number cards and a place-value chart with decimal places. Have each student place four cards on the chart to form a decimal number.

Direct pairs to compare numbers. The player with the greatest number scores a point. Play continues until one student scores 5 points.

Compare Decimals

Use a place-value chart to compare numbers. Circle the correct statement.

ones	.	tenths	hundredths	thousandths
0	.	4		
0	.	6		

0.4 is greater than 0.6.

0.4 is less than 0.6.

ones	.	tenths	hundredths	thousandths
0	.	5	8	
0	.	5	9	

0.58 is greater than 0.59.

0.58 is less than 0.59.

ones	.	tenths	hundredths	thousandths
0	.	0	7	3
0	.	0	1	3

0.073 is greater than 0.013.

0.073 is less than 0.013.

ones	.	tenths	hundredths	thousandths
0	.	5	1	2
0	.	3	1	2

0.512 is greater than 0.312.

0.512 is less than 0.312.

 Tell how you use place value to compare numbers.

Compare Decimals

Use a place-value chart to compare numbers.
Write >, <, or = to complete each statement.

> **> is greater than**
>
> **< is less than**
>
> **= is equal to**

ones	.	tenths	hundredths	thousandths
3	.	0		
3	.	5		

3.0 ◯ 3.5

ones	.	tenths	hundredths	thousandths
2	.	7	6	
2	.	6	7	

2.76 ◯ 2.67

ones	.	tenths	hundredths	thousandths
1	.	0	0	8
1	.	1	0	8

1.008 ◯ 1.108

ones	.	tenths	hundredths	thousandths
4	.	9	5	
4	.	9	5	

4.95 ◯ 4.95

 Tell how you know when two numbers are equal.

Compare Decimals

Use the symbols for greater than (>) or less than (<) to compare the numbers in the place-value chart.

ones	.	tenths	hundredths	thousandths
8	.	9	2	
8	.	9		
8	.	0	9	2
9	.	0	8	9

1

8.92 ◯ 8.9

2

8.9 ◯ 9.089

3

8.9 ◯ 8.092

4

8.092 ◯ 8.92

☆ **Tell how you use a place-value chart to compare numbers.**

Compare Decimals

Compare. Write >, <, or = .

> is greater than; < is less than; = is equal to

 1

4.81 ◯ 4.18

4.18 ◯ 4.81

 2

3.05 ◯ 3.5

3.5 ◯ 3.05

 3

7.20 ◯ 7.2

 4

6.92 ◯ 9.26

☆ **Tell how you compare numbers that have a different number of places.**

Assessment

Use a place-value chart to compare numbers. Write >, <, or = to complete each statement.

ones	.	tenths	hundredths	thousandths
8	.	6	2	
8	.	2	6	

8.62 ◯ 8.26

ones	.	tenths	hundredths	thousandths
4	.	7	2	
7	.	4	2	

4.72 ◯ 7.42

Compare. Use >, <, or =.

5.09 ◯ 5.090

6.35 ◯ 6.3

 **Tell how you know which number is greater.**

Overview   Round Decimals

Directions and Sample Answers for Activity Pages

Day 1	See "Model the Skill" below.
Day 2	Read the directions aloud. Review with students how to locate the number on the number line. Then remind students to determine which tenth the number is closer to. Have students check their work by looking at the digit in the hundredths place to determine whether the tenths place remains the same or if it increases by one. (**1.** 8.5; **2.** 19.1; **3.** 5.2; **4.** 61.9)
Day 3	Read the directions aloud. Encourage students to use their understanding of place value and the number lines to determine each rounded number. Students should see that they can look at the digit in the thousandths place to determine whether the digit in the hundredths place stays the same or increases by one. (**1.** 3.46; **2.** 0.30; **3.** 40.26; **4.** 81.40)
Day 4	Read the directions aloud. Point out that students will round the same number in three different ways. Encourage students to circle the digit they are using to determine whether the digit to its left stays the same or increases by one. (**1.** 5.14, 5.1, 5; **2.** 63.25, 63.3, 63; **3.** 19.68, 19.7, 20)
Day 5	Read the directions aloud. Observe as students complete the page. Do students use place value to round numbers? Do they round up when the digit to the right of the rounding place is 5 or greater? Use your observations to plan further instruction and review. (**1.** 54.4; **2.** 6.91; **3.** 34; **4.** 29.5)

Model the Skill

◆ Hand out the Day 1 activity page.

◆ **Ask:** *How can you use a number line to help you round numbers?* (Find the number on the line and see which whole number it is closer to.) *How can you find 4.2 on the number line?* (Find 4 and move two marks to the right.) Guide students to make a dot where 4.2 is on the number line and determine which whole number it is closer to. (4)

◆ **Say:** *You can also round numbers by looking at the digit to the right of the digit you are rounding to. When rounding to the nearest whole number, which digit will you look at?* (the one in the tenths place) *What digit is in the tenths place of 4.2?* (2) Review with students that if a digit is less than 5, the digit you are rounding to stays the same. If it is 5 or greater, the digit you are rounding to increases by one.

Spin and Round

Use a six-section spinner labeled with the numbers
0, 2, 4, 5, 7, and 8.

Spin the spinner four times and write a number with up to three decimal places.

Explain how to round the number to the nearest whole number, tenth, or hundredth.

◆ Help students complete the activity page by using the number line to round each number to the nearest whole number. Have them also explain how to round the same number just by looking at the digit in the tenths place. (**2.** 38; **3.** 25; **4.** 5)

Round Decimals

Round each number to the nearest whole number. Use the number line to help.

1

4.2 rounds to _____

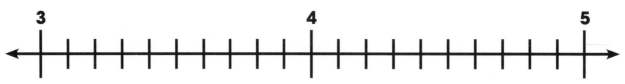

2

37.8 rounds to _____

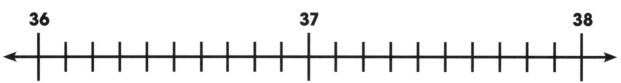

3

24.6 rounds to _____

4

5.0 rounds to _____

 Tell how to use a number line to round decimals to the nearest whole number.

Round Decimals

Round each number to the nearest tenth. Use the number line to help.

8.53 rounds to _____

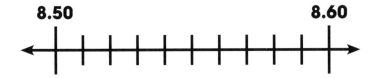

8.50   **8.60**

19.06 rounds to _____

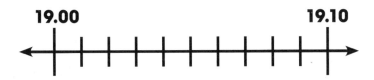

19.00   **19.10**

5.21 rounds to _____

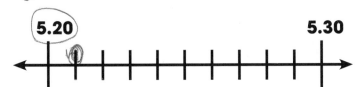

5.20   **5.30**

61.89 rounds to _____

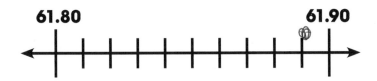

61.80   **61.90**

☆ **Tell how to use place value to round to the nearest tenth.**

Round Decimals

Round each number to the nearest hundredth. Use the number line to help.

 1

3.459 rounds to _____

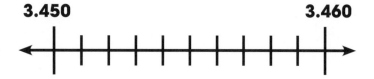

 2

0.295 rounds to _____

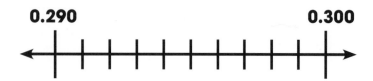

 3

40.261 rounds to _____

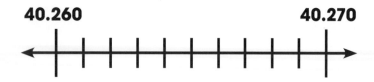

 4

81.403 rounds to _____

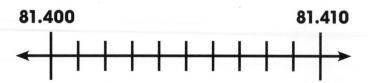

☆ **Tell how rounding to the nearest hundredth is like rounding to the nearest tenth.**

Round Decimals

Round each number in three ways—to the nearest hundredth, the nearest tenth, and the nearest whole number.

5.142

nearest hundredth _____

nearest tenth _____

nearest whole number _____

63.254

nearest hundredth _____

nearest tenth _____

nearest whole number _____

19.678

nearest hundredth _<u>19.680</u>__

nearest tenth _<u>19.700</u>__

nearest whole number _<u>20.00</u>__

⭐ **Tell how rounding to any place is similar.**

Assessment

Solve each problem.

 1

54.43 rounded to the nearest tenth is _____

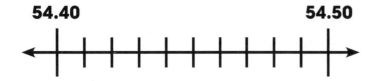

54.40   **54.50**

 2

6.907 rounded to the nearest hundredth is _____

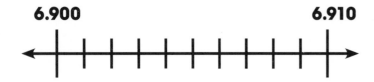

6.900   **6.910**

 3

33.618 rounded to the nearest whole number is _____

 4

29.527 rounded to the nearest tenth is _____

☆ **Tell how you solved the problem.**

Overview   Multiply Whole Numbers

Directions and Sample Answers for Activity Pages

Day 1	See "Model the Skill" below.
Day 2	Tell students that today they will be multiplying 3-digit numbers. Point out that the method is the same. Discuss regrouping and how to record it in multiplication. Guide students through the first problem, talking through the steps, as they multiply ones, tens, and hundreds. For Problem 3, be sure students understand how to multiply when there is a 0 in the factor. (**1.** 612; **2.** 567; **3.** 1,535; **4.** 1,428)
Day 3	Read the directions aloud. Point out that all the problems on the page involve multiplying 2 two-digit numbers. Guide students through the first problem, reminding them to first multiply by the ones digit, starting with the ones and then moving to the tens. Then guide students to multiply by the tens digit. Watch that students align the digits of the partial products correctly when adding to find the final product. (**1.** 546; **2.** 1,188; **3.** 372; **4.** 1,500)
Day 4	Read the directions aloud. Explain that the problems on this page involve regrouping. Remind students to begin with the ones and then move to the tens. Guide students to cross out regrouped tens from finding the first partial product before finding the second partial product. (**1.** 858; **2.** 3,150; **3.** 954; **4.** 4,320)
Day 5	Read the directions aloud. Observe as students complete the page. Do students remember to line up the partial products correctly? Do they remember to add the regrouped amounts? Use your observations to plan further instruction and review. (**1.** 232; **2.** 528; **3.** 448; **4.** 4,263)

Model the Skill

◆ Hand out the Day 1 activity page.

◆ **Say:** *There are different methods to use to multiply numbers. Today we are going to focus on the short form. Just as in addition and subtraction, we begin with the ones column when multiplying. How many ones are there in two groups of 4?* (8) Point out how the number of ones is shown in the ones column of the product. **Ask:** *How many tens are in two groups of 10?* (2) Guide students to write the number of tens in the tens column of the product. **Ask:** *What is the product of 2 and 14?* (28)

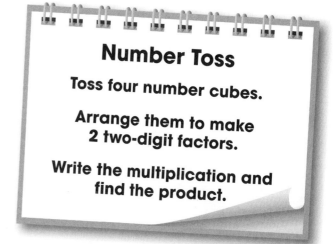

Number Toss

Toss four number cubes.

Arrange them to make 2 two-digit factors.

Write the multiplication and find the product.

◆ Have students look at problem 2. **Ask:** *What do you need to do first to find the product of 32 and 6?* (Multiply the ones—2 x 6 = 12.) *How should we record 12 ones?* Guide students to regroup as 1 ten and 2 ones, recording the 2 ones as part of the answer and the 1 ten as a carry number. Have students multiply tens, reminding them to add the regrouped ten. Help students record the product (192) and understand that it represents (6 x 30) + (6 x 2).

◆ Help students complete the activity page. (**3.** 189; **4.** 235)

Multiply Whole Numbers

Find the product for each problem.

①

2 x 14

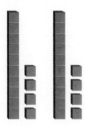

Multiply the ones.

$$\begin{array}{r} 1\boxed{4} \\ \times\ \ \boxed{2} \\ \hline 8 \end{array}$$ ← (2 x 4 = 8)

Multiply the tens.

$$\begin{array}{r} \boxed{1}4 \\ \times\ \ \boxed{2} \\ \hline \square 8 \end{array}$$ ← (2 x 10 = 20)

②

6 x 32

Multiply the ones.

$$\begin{array}{r} {}^{1} \\ 3\boxed{2} \\ \times\ \ \boxed{6} \\ \hline 2 \end{array}$$ ← Regroup 12 ones as 1 ten and 2 ones.
← (6 x 2 = 12)

Multiply the tens.

$$\begin{array}{r} {}^{1} \\ \boxed{3}2 \\ \times\ \ \boxed{6} \\ \hline \square\square 2 \end{array}$$ ← (6 x 30 + 10)

③

3 x 63

$$\begin{array}{r} 63 \\ \times\ \ 3 \\ \hline \end{array}$$

Think:

(3 x ___) + (3 x ___)

④

5 x 47

$$\begin{array}{r} 47 \\ \times\ \ 5 \\ \hline \end{array}$$

☆ **Tell how you found the product.**

Multiply Whole Numbers

Find the product for each problem.

 1

4 x 153

> Think:
> Add the regrouped ten.

> Think:
> Add the regrouped hundreds.

Multiply the ones.
Regroup if possible.

```
    1
  15⌐3⌐
x   ⌐4⌐   ← (4 x 3 = 12)
─────
    8
```

Multiply the tens.
Regroup if possible.

```
  2 1
  1⌐5⌐3
x   ⌐4⌐   ← (4 x 50 + 10)
─────
   12
```

Multiply the hundreds.

```
  2 1
 ⌐1⌐53
x  ⌐4⌐   ← (4 x 100 + 200)
─────
 ☐12
```

 2

3 x 189

```
  189
x   3
```

3

5 x 307

```
  307
x   5
```

 4

6 x 238

```
  238
x   6
```

☆ **Tell why you might need to add to find a product.**

Multiply Whole Numbers

Find the product for each problem.

1

42 x 13

> Think:
> (3 x 2) + (3 x 40)

> Think:
> (10 x 2) + (10 x 40)

```
  42
x 13  ◄ Multiply by the
 126      ones digit.
```

```
  42
x 13  ◄ Multiply by the tens
 126      digit. (10 x 42)
+ 420 ◄ Add the partial products.
```

2

22 x 54

```
   54
 x 22  ◄ Multiply by the
  108      ones digit.
```

> Think:
> (20 x 4) + (20 x 50)

```
   54
 x 22
  108
 +___
```

3

12 x 31

```
   31
 x 12
```

4

25 x 60

```
   60
 x 25
```

 Tell how you used place value.

Multiply Whole Numbers

Find the product for each problem.

1

26 x 33

$$\begin{array}{r} \overset{1}{\boxed{33}} \\ \times\ 2\boxed{6} \\ \hline 198 \end{array}$$ ← Multiply by the ones digit.

$$\begin{array}{r} \boxed{33} \\ \times\ \boxed{26} \\ \hline 198 \\ +\ 660 \end{array}$$ ← Add the partial products.

2

Think:
(40 x 5) + (40 x 70)

42 x 75

$$\begin{array}{r} \overset{1}{75} \\ \times\ 42 \\ \hline 150 \end{array}$$ ← Multiply by the ones digit.

$$\begin{array}{r} 75 \\ \times\ 42 \\ \hline 150 \\ +\ \underline{} \end{array}$$ ← Multiply by the tens digit. Regroup and add.

← Add the partial products.

3

18 x 53

$$\begin{array}{r} 53 \\ \times\ 18 \\ \hline \end{array}$$

4

45 x 96

$$\begin{array}{r} 96 \\ \times\ 45 \\ \hline \end{array}$$

☆ **Tell how you regroup.**

Assessment

Find the product for each problem. Show your work.

4 x 58   58
                        x   4

3 x 176   176
                        x   3

14 x 32   32
                        x 14

49 x 87   87
                        x 49

☆ **Tell how you solved the problem.**

Overview Divide by a One-Digit Divisor

Directions and Sample Answers for Activity Pages

Day 1	See "Model the Skill" below.
Day 2	Read the directions aloud. Guide students through each step of the long division in problem 1. Remind them to start dividing at the tens place. Encourage students to use the worked problem to determine the steps to follow. (**1.** 24; **2.** 13; **3.** 21; **4.** 27)
Day 3	Read the directions aloud. Help students work through each step of the long division, giving extra attention to explaining the second step. Emphasize the importance of vertically aligning the digits in each step. (**1.** 242; **2.** 125; **3.** 141; **4.** 118)
Day 4	Read the directions aloud. Point out that the divisor is greater than the digit in the hundreds place, so students need to look at both the hundreds and tens places when deciding which digit to write in the quotient. Encourage students to think of multiplication facts to determine the digits on the quotient. Remind them to align the digits of the quotient above the appropriate digit in the dividend. (**1.** 69; **2.** 89; **3.** 42; **4.** 83)
Day 5	Read the directions aloud. Observe as students complete the page. Do students demonstrate how to use long division? Do they divide, multiply, and subtract accurately? Use your observations to plan further instruction and review. (**1.** 7; **2.** 38; **3.** 126; **4.** 99)

Model the Skill

◆ Hand out the Day 1 activity page.

◆ **Ask:** *What does problem 1 use to show the division?* (an array) *What is the dividend?* (27) *How is the divisor shown in the array?* (by the number of rows) *How can you use the array to find the quotient?* (Possible answer: Count the number of counters in each row.) Guide students to see that the number of rows is the divisor and the number of columns is the quotient. **Ask:** *What is the quotient of 27 divided by 3?* (9)

◆ **Ask:** *What does problem 2 use to show the division?* (an area model) *What is the dividend?* (24) *How are the divisor and quotient shown in the area model?* (The 4 rows show the divisor while the 6 columns show the quotient.) *What is the quotient of 24 divided by 4?* (6) Discuss with students how the area model shows the multiplication 4 times 6.

◆ **Ask:** *How can you use multiplication to check division?* (Possible answer: Multiply the quotient by the divisor and see if you get the dividend.)

◆ Help students complete the activity page, using counters or grid paper to model the division and draw a picture. (**3.** 3; **4.** 6)

Use Manipulatives

Use counters or cubes equivalent to the dividend.

Arrange them in the number of rows indicated by the divisor.

Find the number of counters or cubes in each row to determine the quotient.

Divide by a One-Digit Divisor

Find the quotient for each problem. Draw a picture.

1 27 ÷ 3

← quotient

3) 27‾

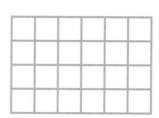

2 24 ÷ 4

← quotient

4) 24‾

3 18 ÷ 6

← quotient

6) 18‾

4 30 ÷ 5

← quotient

5) 30‾

☆ **Tell how you can use multiplication to check your answer.**

Divide by a One-Digit Divisor

Divide. Show your work.

1   96 ÷ 4 = _____

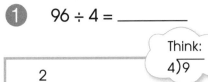

2 4) 96 ← Divide tens. 80 Then multiply. (20 x 4 = 80)	2 4) 96 – 80 ← Subtract. (96 – 80 = 16) 16 ← Divide ones.	24 4) 96 – 80 16 – 16 ← Multiply. (4 x 4 = 16) 0 ← Subtract. (16 – 16 = 0)

Think:
 4) 9

Think:
 4) 16

2   78 ÷ 6   6) 78

3   63 ÷ 3   3) 63

4   54 ÷ 2   2) 54

☆ **Tell how you solved the problem.**

Divide by a One-Digit Divisor

Divide. Show your work.

1 726 ÷ 3 = _____

2 3)726 ← Divide hundreds. −600 ← Multiply. 126 ← Then subtract.	24 3)726 − 600 126 ← Divide tens. − 120 ← Multiply. 6 ← Then subtract.	24_ 3)726 − 600 126 − 120 6 ← Divide ones. −____ ← Multiply. ← Subtract.

Think:
3)12

2 625 ÷ 5

```
      1
  5 )625
   - 500
```

3 564 ÷ 4

```
      1
  4 )564
   - 400
```

4 944 ÷ 8

```
  8 )944
```

⭐ **Tell the steps you took to find the quotient.**

Unit 9 • Mathematics Intervention Activities Grade 5 • © 2014 Newmark Learning, LLC

Divide by a One-Digit Divisor

Divide. Show your work.

1 414 ÷ 6 = _____

```
        6
   6 )414   ◄ Not enough hundreds.
    - 360      Divide tens.
      54
```

Think:
6 x ? = 41 or less

2 623 ÷ 7 = _____

```
        8
   3 )623
    - 560
```

Think:
7 x ? = 62 or less

3 126 ÷ 3 = _____

```
   3 )126
```

4 415 ÷ 5 = _____

```
   5 )415
```

⭐ **Tell how you know where to place the first digit in the quotient.**

Assessment

Solve each problem. Show your work.

1 56 ÷ 8 = _____

$$8 \overline{)\, 56}$$

---

2 76 ÷ 2 = _____

$$2 \overline{)\, 76}$$

---

3 504 ÷ 4 = _____

$$4 \overline{)\, 504}$$

---

4 693 ÷ 7 = _____

$$7 \overline{)\, 693}$$

☆ **Tell the steps you took to find the quotient.**

Overview   Divide by a Two-Digit Divisor

Directions and Sample Answers for Activity Pages

Day 1	See "Model the Skill" below.
Day 2	Read the directions aloud. Guide students through the steps of problem 1, pointing out how 18 of something cannot be divided into 21 groups because 21 is greater than 18. Encourage students to use their basic facts to help them decide on the quotient. Check that students are multiplying the quotient by the divisor to see that it equals the dividend. (**1.** 9; **2.** 6; **3.** 8; **4.** 7)
Day 3	Read the directions aloud. Help students work through each step of the long division. Remind them to think of basic facts and use their knowledge of number order to decide which numbers to place in the quotient. Point out that they may have to change the quotient if their estimate is too great. (**1.** 29; **2.** 22; **3.** 30; **4.** 17)
Day 4	Read the directions aloud. Guide students through the steps of problem 1, emphasizing the need for a zero in the quotient as outlined in the second step. Remind students to align the digits of the quotient above the appropriate digit in the dividend. (**1.** 206; **2.** 37; **3.** 410)
Day 5	Read the directions aloud. Observe as students complete the page. Do students divide and multiply by two-digit numbers accurately? Do they align the digits of the quotient appropriately? Use your observations to plan further instruction and review. (**1.** 5; **2.** 9; **3.** 19; **4.** 206)

Model the Skill

◆ Hand out the Day 1 activity page.

◆ **Say:** *The problems on this page show a two-digit dividend and a two-digit divisor. You can think of basic facts to help you decide what number to use in the quotient.* Guide students to use the digits in the tens places of the dividend and divisor to decide what number to write in the quotient. **Ask:** *What is 4 divided by 1?* (4) **Say:** *Write the quotient above the ones place because the divisor has two digits.* **Ask:** *What is 4 times 12?* (48) Guide students to write the product below the dividend and subtract to see that the answer is correct. **Ask:** *What is the quotient of 48 divided by 12?* (4)

◆ **Ask:** *What basic fact can you think about for problem 2?* (4 ÷ 2) *What should I write as the quotient?* (2) *Where should I write it?* (above the 6) *How do I check my answer?* (multiply 2 by 23)

◆ Help students complete the activity page by looking at the tens places in the dividends and divisors and using basic facts to find the quotients. (**3.** 3; **4.** 4)

Multiply and Then Divide

Have pairs of students each toss two number cubes to generate 2 two-digit numbers.

One student multiplies the numbers together to find the product. That same student writes a division expression using the product as the dividend and one of the factors as the divisor. The partner then solves the division. Students check to see that the quotient matches the other factor.

Divide by a Two-Digit Divisor

Find the quotient for each problem. Think about basic facts.

1 48 ÷ 12

$$\begin{array}{r} 4 \\ 12\overline{)48} \end{array}$$ ← Divide tens.

_____ ← Multiply.

← Subtract.

> Think of a basic fact.
> 4 ÷ 1 = ?

2 46 ÷ 23

$$23\overline{)46}$$

3 99 ÷ 33

$$33\overline{)99}$$

4 84 ÷ 21

$$21\overline{)84}$$

☆ **Tell how you can use basic facts to find the quotient.**

Divide by a Two-Digit Divisor

Divide. Show your work.

1 189 ÷ 21 = _____

Decide where
to place the
first digit.

21) 189 ← Look at tens.
21 > 18
There are no tens
or hundreds in the
quotient.

Think:
180 ÷ 21 = ?

        9
21) 189 ← Divide.
  - 189 ← Multiply.
         ← Subtract.

2 528 ÷ 88 = _____

88) 528

3 120 ÷ 15 = _____

15) 120

4 266 ÷ 38 = _____

38) 266

⭐ **Tell how you can use multiplication to check your answer.**

Divide by a Two-Digit Divisor

Divide. Show your work.

1   435 ÷ 15 = _____

Divide	Adjust	Continue Dividing
$$\begin{array}{r} 3 \\ 15\overline{)435} \\ -\;450 \end{array}$$ ← Try 3. 450 > 435 3 is too great.	$$\begin{array}{r} 2 \\ 15\overline{)435} \\ -\;300 \\ \hline 135 \end{array}$$ ← Try 2. ← Multiply. (20 x 15) ← Then subtract.	$$\begin{array}{r} 29 \\ 15\overline{)435} \\ -\;300 \\ \hline 135 \\ -\;135 \\ \hline 0 \end{array}$$ **Think:** 135 ÷ 15 = ? ← Try 9. ← Multiply and subtract.

2   968 ÷ 44 = _____

$$\begin{array}{r} 2 \\ 44\overline{)968} \\ -\;880 \end{array}$$

3   720 ÷ 24 = _____

$$24\overline{)720}$$

4   952 ÷ 56 = _____

$$56\overline{)952}$$

☆ **Tell about what strategies you used to find the quotient.**

    Unit 10 • Mathematics Intervention Activities Grade 5 • © 2014 Newmark Learning, LLC

Divide by a Two-Digit Divisor

Divide. Show your work.

1   9,476 ÷ 46 = _____

Divide the hundreds.	Divide the tens.	Divide the ones.
$$\begin{array}{r} 2 \\ 46\overline{)9476} \end{array}$$ ← Think: 94 ÷ 46 − 9200 ← Multiply. (200 x 46) 276 ← Subtract.	$$\begin{array}{r} 20 \\ 46\overline{)9476} \end{array}$$ − 9200 276 ← Think: 276 ÷ 46 27 < 46, so write 0 in the quotient.	$$\begin{array}{r} 20 \\ 46\overline{)9476} \end{array}$$ − 9200 Think: 276 ÷ 46 276 ← Try 6 − _____ ← Multiply. ← Subtract.

2   2,072 ÷ 56 = _____

$$\begin{array}{r} 3 \\ 56\overline{)2072} \end{array}$$ ← Think: 20 ÷ 56 − 9200 20 < 56 276 There are no hundreds or thousands in the quotients.	$$\begin{array}{r} 3 \\ 56\overline{)2072} \end{array}$$ Divide. ← Think: 207 ÷ 56. − 1680 ← Multiply. (30 x 56) 392 ← Subract.	$$\begin{array}{r} 3 \\ 56\overline{)2072} \end{array}$$ − 1680 392 ← Divide. − _____ ← Multiply. ← Subtract.

3   9,020 ÷ 22 = _____

$$22\overline{)9020}$$

☆ **Tell how you know where to write the number in the quotient.**

Assessment

Solve each problem. Show your work.

1 60 ÷ 12 = _____

$$12\overline{)60}$$

_____

2 216 ÷ 24 = _____

$$24\overline{)216}$$

_____

3 855 ÷ 45 = _____

$$45\overline{)855}$$

_____

4 9,476 ÷ 46 = _____

$$46\overline{)9476}$$

☆ **Tell how you know where to align the digits when writing the quotient.**

Overview   Add and Subtract Decimals

Directions and Sample Answers for Activity Pages

Day 1	See "Model the Skill" below.
Day 2	Read the directions aloud. Point out the addends shown in the place-value chart in problem 1, noting that the decimals are aligned. Remind students to add starting on the right and to include a decimal point in the sum. Encourage students to use the place-value chart in problem 2 and to write the addends in vertical form in problems 3 and 4. (**1.** 88.14; **2.** 43.51; **3.** 8.77; **4.** 15.11)
Day 3	Read the directions aloud. Walk students through the use of the models in problems 1 and 2 by crossing out the amount that is being subtracted. Remind students to subtract beginning on the right and to make sure that the answer includes a decimal point. Encourage students to use addition to check their subtraction. (**1.** 0.24; **2.** 0.79; **3.** 0.14; **4.** 0.29)
Day 4	Read the directions aloud. Point out the zero in the hundredths place in the problem 1 chart. It holds a place and indicates the need for regrouping. Encourage students to use the place-value charts in problems 1 and 2 and to write problems 3 and 4 vertically. Remind students to subtract starting on the right and to include a decimal point in their answer. (**1.** 1.32; **2.** 3.16; **3.** 3.9; **4.** 5.46)
Day 5	Read the directions aloud. Observe as students complete the page. Do students add or subtract starting on the right? Do they align the decimals when they write the problem vertically? Use your observations to plan further instruction and review. (**1.** 0.41; **2.** 0.53; **3.** 11.67; **4.** 6.28)

Model the Skill

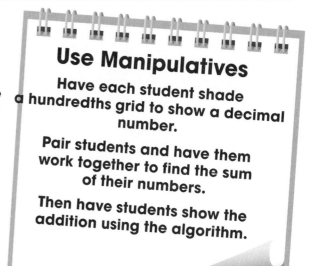

Use Manipulatives

Have each student shade a hundredths grid to show a decimal number.

Pair students and have them work together to find the sum of their numbers.

Then have students show the addition using the algorithm.

◆ Hand out the Day 1 activity page and base-ten blocks (tens and ones).

◆ Display a hundreds flat. **Say:** *Today we are going to see this as one whole. If this is one, what is a tens rod?* (one-tenth) *What is a ones cube?* (one-hundredth) Have students look at the pictured models in problem 1 on the activity sheet. Discuss how the models match the decimals in the expression. **Ask:** *What is the sum of the two sets of models?* (six-tenths and twelve-hundredths) Guide students to regroup to determine a total of seven-tenths and two-hundredths, or seventy-two hundredths.

◆ Point to the vertical addition. **Ask:** *How do you add whole numbers?* (Add the columns starting on the right.) Guide students to add the decimals, starting with the hundredths place and regrouping as needed. **Say:** *The decimal points are lined up. Write a decimal point in the same position in the sum.* (0.72)

◆ **Say:** *Problem 2 shows the decimals on hundredths grids.* **Ask:** *Why are there 90 squares shaded on the second grid when the number is nine-tenths?* (Possible answer: 9 tenths and 90 hundredths are the same.) Lead students in using the grids to add. Point out that the decimals are aligned in the vertical addition. **Say:** *A zero has been added to the second addend to hold the place.* Guide students to add the decimals from right to left, regrouping as needed. **Say:** *When you combined the models, you got a sum greater than 1. What sum did you get?* (1.42)

◆ Help students complete the activity page, using base-ten blocks or grid paper to model the addition. (**3.** 0.91; **4.** 1.11)

Add and Subtract Decimals

Find the sum for each problem. Use models or draw a picture.

1   0.45 + 0.27

       0.45
     + 0.27
     ‾‾‾‾‾‾

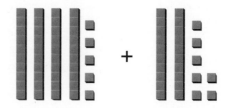

---

2   0.52 + 0.9

       0.52
     + 0.90
     ‾‾‾‾‾‾

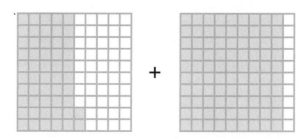

---

3   0.13 + 0.78

       0.13
     + 0.78
     ‾‾‾‾‾‾

---

4   0.81 + 0.3

       0.81
     + 0.3
     ‾‾‾‾‾‾

☆ **Tell how you can use models to add decimals.**

Add and Subtract Decimals

Find the sum for each problem.

1 72.8 + 15.34 = _____

	tens	ones	.	tenths	hundredths
	7	2	.	8	
+	1	5	.	3	4

2 39.71 + 3.8 = _____

	tens	ones	.	tenths	hundredths
+					

3 5.07 + 3.7 = _____

4 14.32 + 0.79 = _____

⭐ **Tell how you can use a place-value chart to add decimals.**

Add and Subtract Decimals

Find the difference for each problem. Use models or draw a picture.

1 0.56 – 0.32

$$
\begin{array}{r}
0.56 \\
-\ 0.32 \\
\hline
\end{array}
$$

2 0.9 – 0.11

$$
\begin{array}{r}
0.90 \\
-\ 0.11 \\
\hline
\end{array}
$$

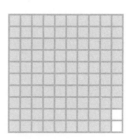

3 0.28 – 0.14

$$
\begin{array}{r}
0.28 \\
-\ 0.14 \\
\hline
\end{array}
$$

4 0.98 – 0.69

$$
\begin{array}{r}
0.98 \\
-\ 0.69 \\
\hline
\end{array}
$$

☆ **Tell how you can use addition to check your subtraction.**

Add and Subtract Decimals

Find the difference for each problem.

1 1.7 – 0.38 = _____

tens	ones	.	tenths	hundredths
	1	.	7	0
+	0	.	3	8

2 15.06 – 11.9 = _____

tens	ones	.	tenths	hundredths
+				

3 4.33 – 0.43 = _____

4 9.08 – 3.62 = _____

☆ **Tell how you subtract decimals.**

Assessment

Solve each problem. Show your work.

① 0.24 + 0.17   0.24
                      + 0.17
                      ‾‾‾‾‾‾

② 0.73 – 0.2   0.73
                      + 0.2
                      ‾‾‾‾‾

③ 49.5 – 37.83 = _____

④ 5.38 + 0.9 = _____

☆ **Tell how you solved the problem.**

Overview   Multiply Decimals

Directions and Sample Answers for Activity Pages

Day 1	See "Model the Skill" below.
Day 2	Read the directions aloud. Walk students through the steps shown in problem 1. Emphasize that the number of decimal places in the factors indicates the number of decimal places in the product. If needed, review with students how to multiply beginning with the digits on the right. (**1.** 1.5; **2.** 1.89; **3.** 2.8; **4.** 4.86)
Day 3	Read the directions aloud. Walk students through the steps shown in problem 1. Point out that both factors are decimals. Emphasize that the total number of decimal places in the factors should be used to determine where to place the decimal point in the product. Note that the decimal points do not need to align in multiplication as they do in addition and subtraction. (**1.** 1.61; **2.** 7.224; **3.** 1.7199; **4.** 0.015)
Day 4	Read the directions aloud. Point out that there are more products listed than there are problems so not all products will be used. Students should realize that they can match by simply counting the number of decimal places in a product and matching it to a problem that has that number of decimal places in its factors. (**1.** 103.5; **2.** 10.08; **3.** 34.017; **4.** 0.0856)
Day 5	Read the directions aloud. Observe as students complete the page. Do students multiply starting on the right? Does the product have the same number of decimal places as the factors? Use your observations to plan further instruction and review. (**1.** 0.12; **2.** 0.35; **3.** 7.461; **4.** 163.654)

Model the Skill

◆ Hand out the Day 1 activity page. Students may wish to use crayons or colored pencils to model the factors on this page.

◆ **Say**: *Today, we are going to multiply decimals using a hundredths grid to model the multiplication. The grid shows one whole.* Ask: *What does each row show?* (one tenth) *What does each column show?* (one tenth) *What two decimals are we multiplying in problem 1?* (0.5 and 0.9) Guide students to see how each factor is shown on the grid. **Ask**: *How many squares are shaded by both factors?* (45) *What decimal names those squares?* (0.45) *What is 5 tenths of 9 tenths?* (45 hundredths)

◆ **Ask**: *How can you show the two factors on the grid in problem 2?* (Possible answer: Shade 6 rows and 7 columns.) Observe as students model the two factors on the grid. **Ask**: *How do you know the product of 0.6 and 0.7?* (See how many squares are shaded for both factors.) *What is the product of 0.6 and 0.7?* (0.42)

◆ Help students complete the activity page by shading the products on the grid. Encourage students to name the number of shaded hundredths and write the decimal that matches. ((3) 0.72 (4) 0.08)

Use Manipulatives

Use a hundredths grid to model the decimals.

Guide students to shade rows to show one factor and columns to show the other factor.

Students should note that the squares that are shaded for both factors show the product.

Name _____

Multiply Decimals

Find each product. Use the grid to help.

 1

$0.5 \times 0.9 =$ _____

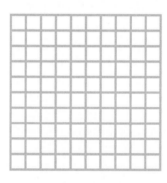

2

$0.6 \times 0.7 =$ _____

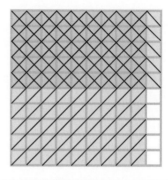

3

$0.8 \times 0.9 =$ _____

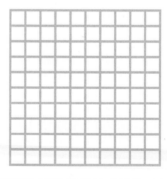

4

$0.4 \times 0.2 =$ _____

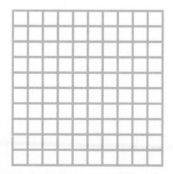

⭐ **Tell how you can use models to multiply decimals.**

Name _____

Multiply Decimals

Find each product. Multiply as you would with whole numbers.

1 0.3 x 5

$$\begin{array}{r} \overset{1}{0.3} \\ \times\ \ 5 \\ \hline 1\ 5 \end{array}$$

← Count the decimal places in the factor.

← Write the decimal point in the product.

Think: 1 decimal place

Think: The number of decimal places in the product equals the total number of decimal places in the factors.

2 0.21 x 9

$$\begin{array}{r} 0.21 \\ \times\ \ \ \ 9 \\ \hline 1.89 \end{array}$$

← 2 decimal places

← 0 decimal places

← Product should have 2 decimal places

3 0.4 x 7

$$\begin{array}{r} 0.4 \\ \times\ \ \ 7 \\ \hline \end{array}$$

← 1 decimal place

← 0 decimal places

4 0.81 x 6

$$\begin{array}{r} 0.81 \\ \times\ \ \ \ 6 \\ \hline \end{array}$$

← 2 decimal places

← 0 decimal places

☆ **Tell how you know how many decimal places should be in the product.**

Name _____

Multiply Decimals

Find each product. Multiply as you would with whole numbers.

1 2.3 x 0.7

$$
\begin{array}{r}
\overset{2}{2}.3 \\
\times\ 0.7 \\
\hline
1\ 6\ 1
\end{array}
$$

← 1 decimal place
← 1 decimal place
← Write the decimal point in the product.

---

2 6.02 x 1.2

$$
\begin{array}{r}
6.02 \\
\times\ 1.2 \\
\end{array}
$$

← 2 decimal places
← 1 decimal places
← Product will have 3 decimal places.

---

3 8.19 x 0.21

$$
\begin{array}{r}
8.19 \\
\times\ 0.21 \\
\end{array}
$$

---

4 0.03 x 0.5

$$
\begin{array}{r}
0.03 \\
\times\ 0.5 \\
\end{array}
$$

☆ **Tell how you found the product.**

   Unit 12 • Mathematics Intervention Activities Grade 5 • © 2014 Newmark Learning, LLC

Multiply Decimals

Match. Draw a line from each problem to its product.

Problems	**Products**

①   34.5
    x   3   0.0856

1,008

②   12.6
    x   0.8   103.5

③   14.79
    x   2.3   10.08

34.017

④   4.28
    x   0.02

856

☆ **Tell how you can match the products without multiplying.**

Assessment

Find the product for each problem. Show your work.

1 0.4 x 0.3

$$\begin{array}{r} .4 \\ \times\ .3 \\ \hline \end{array}$$

2 0.07 x 5

$$\begin{array}{r} 0.07 \\ \times\ \ \ \ 5 \\ \hline \end{array}$$

3 8.29 x 0.9

$$\begin{array}{r} 8.29 \\ \times\ \ \ 0.9 \\ \hline \end{array}$$

4 69.64 x 2.35

$$\begin{array}{r} 96.64 \\ \times\ \ \ 3.35 \\ \hline \end{array}$$

☆ **Tell how you solved the problem.**

Overview   Divide Decimals

Directions and Sample Answers for Activity Pages

Day 1	See "Model the Skill" below.
Day 2	Walk students through the steps shown in problem 1. Point out how to place the decimal point, and why they need to write zero in the ones place in the quotient. Discuss the steps in problem 2, especially noting the 'bring down' step. Remind students to align the digits in the quotient as they divide. (**1.** 0.9; **2.** 5.9; **3.** 0.79; **4.** 1.95)
Day 3	Tell students today they will be dividing numbers that have a zero in the dividend. Discuss each step in problem 1. Be sure students understand 0 x n = 0, so 0 ÷ n = 0. Show students how they can multiply the quotient by the divisor to check their division. The product of the multiplication should match the dividend. (**1.** 4.03; **2.** 0.81; **3.** 5.01; **4.** $8.03)
Day 4	Read the directions aloud. Tell students that sometimes they may need to write zeroes in the dividend to continue dividing. Point out this often occurs when dividing money. Help students complete the page. If students have difficulty aligning the digits, show them how to use lined paper turned vertically. (**1.** 0.12; **2.** 1.25; **3.** $3.92; **4.** 0.25)
Day 5	Read the directions aloud. Observe as students complete the page. Do they place the decimal point in the correct place in the quotient? Can students divide when zeroes are in the dividend. Use your observations to plan further instruction and review. (**1.** 0.53 ; **2.** 0.96; **3.** 2.01; **4.** 2.04)

Model the Skill

◆ Hand out the Day 1 activity page and base-ten blocks.

◆ **Say:** *Today, we are going to divide decimals using base-ten blocks.* Hold up a hundreds flat and explain that it will represent one whole. **Ask:** *What is a tens rod? (one tenth) What is a ones cube? (one hundredth)* Have students look at the pictured models in problem 1 on the activity sheet. Point out how 5 and 4 tenths are shown. **Ask:** *How can you divide 5.4 into two groups?* (Possible answer: Put two wholes into each group, regroup 1 whole as 10 tenths and divide the 14 tenths into two groups of 7 tenths.) *What is 5.4 divided by 2?* (2.7)

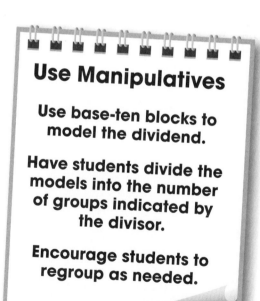

Use Manipulatives

Use base-ten blocks to model the dividend.

Have students divide the models into the number of groups indicated by the divisor.

Encourage students to regroup as needed.

◆ Direct students to problem 2. **Ask:** *How can you divide 2.5 into 5 groups?* (Possible answer: Regroup each whole as 10 tenths so that there are 25 tenths. Then divide the 25 tenths into 5 groups with 5 each.) *What is 2.5 divided by 5?* (0.5)

◆ Help students complete the activity page by showing each dividend with base-ten blocks and dividing the blocks into the number of groups indicated by the divisor. (**3.** 1.53; **4.** 1.34)

Name _____

Divide Decimals

Find each quotient. Use models to help.

① 5.4 ÷ 2 = _____

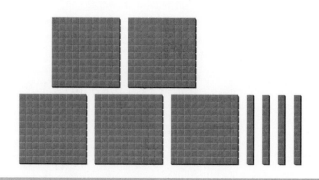

② 2.5 ÷ 5 = _____

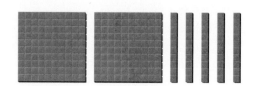

③ 6.12 ÷ 4 = _____

④ 4.02 ÷ 3 = _____

☆ **Tell how you can use models to divide decimals.**

Divide Decimals

Find each quotient. Divide as you would with whole numbers.

1 5.4 ÷ 6 = _____

$$6\overline{)5.4}^{\,.}$$ ← Place the decimal point in the quotient directly above the decimal point in the dividend.

$$6\overline{)5.4}^{\,0.}$$
← Divide. Think: $6\overline{)54}$
- _____ ← Multiply.
← Subtract.

2 41.3 ÷ 7 = _____

$7\overline{)41.3}^{\,.}$ ← Place the decimal point.	$7\overline{)41.3}^{\,5.}$ ← Divide. − 35 ← Multiply. 6 ← Subtract. Think: $7\overline{)41}$	$7\overline{)41.3}^{\,5.\_}$ ← Divide. − 35↓ ← Bring down. 6 3 ← Divide. Think: $7\overline{)63}$

3 6.32 ÷ 8 = _____

$$8\overline{)6.32}$$

Remember: If there are no whole numbers in the quotient, write a zero to show the ones place.

4 9.75 ÷ 5 = _____

$$5\overline{)9.75}$$

⭐ **Tell how you can use multiplication to check your answer.**

Name _____

Divide Decimals

Find each quotient. Divide as you would with whole numbers.

1 8.06 ÷ 2 = _____

Think:
2)8‾

.⟵ Place the decimal point. 2)8.06	4. 2)8.06 ⟵ Divide. — ⟵ Multiply. ⟵ Subtract.	4.0__ 2)8.06 ⟵ Bring down. Divide. - 8 ↓ 0 0↓ 6

Think:
2)0‾ = 0 and 0 x 2 = 0.
Write 0 in the quotient.

Divide 2)6‾

2 4.05 ÷ 5 = _____

8)4.05

3 10.02 ÷ 2 = _____

2)10.02

4 $24.09 ÷ 3 = _____

3)24.09

⭐ **Tell how you know your answer is correct.**

 Unit 13 • Mathematics Intervention Activities Grade 5 • © 2014 Newmark Learning, LLC

Divide Decimals

Find each quotient.

1 1.8 ÷ 15 = _____

Think:
15)‾18‾

0.
15)1.8 ← Place the decimal point. Write zero in the ones place.
	0.1
	15)1.8
	- 15
	    3 ← Divide.
	← Multiply.
	← Subtract.
		0.1_
		15)1.80 ← Write zero in the dividend so you can contiue to divide.
		- 15↓
		    30

Think:
15)‾30‾

2 42.5 ÷ 34 = _____

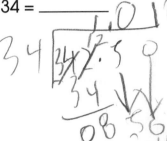

34)42.50 ← Remember to write zero in the dividend. Continue to divide until the remainder is 0.

3 $98 ÷ 25 = _____

25)98

4 4.5 ÷ 18 = _____

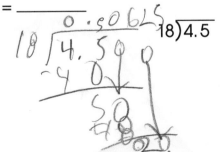

18)4.5

☆ **Tell how you divide with decimals.**

Assessment

Find the quotient for each problem. Show your work.

1 2.12 ÷ 4

$$4\overline{)2.12}$$

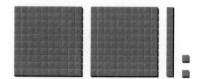

---

2 2.88 ÷ 3

$$3\overline{)2.88}$$

---

3 8.04 ÷ 4

$$4\overline{)8.04}$$

---

4 40.8 ÷ 20

$$20\overline{)40.8}$$

⭐ **Tell how you solved the problem.**

Overview Add Fractions

Directions and Sample Answers for Activity Pages

Day 1	See "Model the Skill" below.
Day 2	Tell students that sometimes they will need to find a common multiple of two denominators in order to find the common denominator. Remind students that they find the multiple of a number by multiplying the number by 1, 2, 3, and so on. Help students complete the page. (**1.** 12, 8/12 + 3/12, 11/12; **2.** 10, 5/5, 6/10 + 5/10 = 11/10 or 1 1/10; **3.** 9, 18, 27; 6, 12, 18; 18; 2/2, 3/3, 4/18 + 6/18 = 10/18 or 5/9; **4.** 13/15)
Day 3	Read the directions aloud. Discuss how to estimate with fractions. Students should think about each fraction in relationship to 1/2. If two fractions are 1/2 or greater, then their sum will be greater than 1. Help students complete the page. (**1.** greater than; **2.** less than; **3.** greater than; **4.** greater than)
Day 4	Read the directions aloud. Tell students that adding mixed numbers is like adding fractions, and that they will need to find a common denominator. Students can write the mixed number as an improper fraction (a fraction greater than 1) before adding. Students may add the fractions and the whole numbers separately, but then they will need to remember to regroup as necessary. (**1.** 2 1/4; **2.** 6/9, 15/9, 2 1/9; **3.** 3/12, 4/12, 27/12, 16/12, 3 7/12; **4.** 2 7/8)
Day 5	Read the directions aloud. Observe as students complete the page. Do students demonstrate how to add unlike fractions? Can they find a common denominator and write an equivalent fraction? Do they write the sum in simplest form? Use your observations to plan further instruction and review. (**1.** 6/10 or 3/5; **2.** 4, 8, 12, 16, 20; 5, 10, 15, 20; 20; 5/5, 4/4, 15/20 + 8/20 = 23/20 or 1 3/20; **3.** 11/6, 2/2, 4/6, 15/6 or 2 3/6 or 2 1/2; **4.** 3)

Model the Skill

◆ Hand out the Day 1 activity page.

◆ **Say:** *Today we are going to add fractions.* Write *1/5 + 2/5* on the board. **Ask:** *How do we add fractions that have the same denominator?* (add the numerators) Have students look at problem 1 and discuss how they might add the fractions when the denominators are different.

◆ **Ask:** *What can we do to write these fractions with a common denominator—denominators that are the same? How can we use equivalent fractions?* Help students understand that when one denominator is a multiple of the other denominator, they can simply write an equivalent fraction. Review how to find equivalent fractions by multiplying (1/3 x 2/2 = 2/6) or dividing.

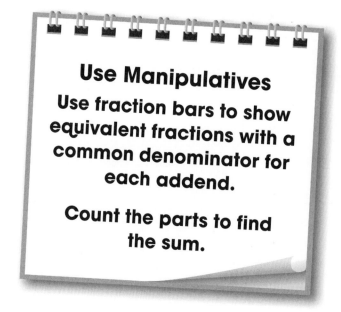

Use Manipulatives

Use fraction bars to show equivalent fractions with a common denominator for each addend.

Count the parts to find the sum.

◆ Help students complete the activity page. Have them use the art to show addition. You may wish to have students use equivalent fractions to write the sum in simplest form. Be sure they understand that a fraction is in simplest form when 1 is the only number that divides both the numerator and denominator. (**1.** 2/6, 3/6 or 1/2; **2.** 2/8 + 2/8 = 4/8 or 1/2; **3.** 3/6, 4/6 or 2/3; **4.** 3/8)

Add Fractions

Write an equivalent fraction. Then find the sum.

1

$\dfrac{1}{3}$ $=$ $\dfrac{\square}{6}$

$+\ \dfrac{1}{6}$ $+\ \dfrac{1}{6}$

2

$\dfrac{2}{8}$ $=$ $\dfrac{\square}{\square}$

$+\ \dfrac{1}{4}$ $+\ \dfrac{\square}{8}$

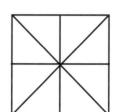

3

$\dfrac{1}{2}$

$+\ \dfrac{1}{6}$

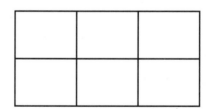

---

4   Ashley planted tomatoes in $\frac{1}{4}$ of the garden.
She planted hot peppers in $\frac{1}{8}$ of the garden.
How much of the garden did she plant?

$\dfrac{1}{4} + \dfrac{1}{8} = ?$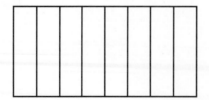

_____ of the garden

☆ **Tell how you add fractions.**

Add Fractions

Find a common denominator. Add.

1 multiples of 3: 3, 6, 9, 12, 15

multiples of 4: 4, 8, 12, 16   The least common multiple of 3 and 4 is ___.

$$\begin{array}{ccccc} \frac{2}{3} & & \frac{2}{3} \times \frac{4}{4} & & \frac{\square}{12} \\ = & & & = & \\ +\frac{1}{4} & & \frac{1}{4} \times \frac{3}{3} & & +\frac{\square}{12} \\ \hline \_\_\_\_ & & & & \_\_\_\_ \end{array}$$

$\rangle$ The least common denominator is 12.

---

2 multiples of 5: 5, 10, 15

multiples of 2: 2, 4, 6, 8, 10, 12   The least common multiple of 5 and 2 is ___.

$$\begin{array}{ccccc} \frac{3}{5} & & \frac{3}{5} \times \frac{2}{2} & & \frac{\square}{\square} \\ = & & & = & \\ +\frac{1}{2} & & \frac{1}{2} \times \frac{\square}{\square} & & +\frac{\square}{\square} \\ \hline \_\_\_\_ & & & & \_\_\_\_ \end{array}$$

---

3 multiples of 9: ___, ___, ___

multiples of 6: ___, ___, ___   The least common multiple of 9 and 6 is ___.

$$\begin{array}{ccccc} \frac{2}{9} & & \frac{2}{9} \times \frac{\square}{\square} & & \frac{\square}{\square} \\ = & & & = & \\ +\frac{2}{6} & & \frac{2}{6} \times \frac{\square}{\square} & & +\frac{\square}{\square} \\ \hline \_\_\_\_ & & & & \_\_\_\_ \end{array}$$

---

4 Jake read $\frac{1}{5}$ of a book in a week. He read another $\frac{2}{3}$ of the book the next week. How much of the book has he read?

$$\frac{1}{5} + \frac{2}{3} = n$$

_____ of the book

⭐ **Tell how you solved the problem.**

Add Fractions

Estimate the sum. Write "greater than" or "less than" to complete each sentence.

 1

$$\frac{2}{4} + \frac{5}{8}$$

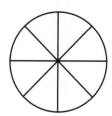

The sum will be _____ 1.

 2

$$\frac{2}{5} + \frac{3}{10} = \text{_____}$$

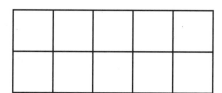

The sum will be _____ 1.

 3

$$\frac{5}{7} + \frac{6}{8} = \text{_____}$$

The sum will be _____ 1.

 4

$$\frac{1}{6} + \frac{6}{10} = \text{_____}$$

The sum will be _____ $\frac{1}{2}$.

⭐ **Tell how you estimate.**

Add Fractions

Find the sum for each problem. Write the sum as a mixed number.

1 $1\frac{1}{2}$ = $1\frac{2}{4}$ = $\frac{6}{4}$

   $+\ \frac{3}{4}$ $+\ \frac{3}{4}$

$1\frac{1}{2} + \frac{3}{4} =$ _____

2 $1\frac{2}{3}$ = $1\frac{\square}{9}$ = $\frac{\square}{9}$

   $+\ \frac{4}{9}$ $+\ \frac{4}{9}$

$1\frac{2}{3} + \frac{4}{9} =$ _____

3 $2\frac{1}{4}$ = $2\frac{\square}{\square}$ = $\frac{\square}{\square}$

   $+\ 1\frac{1}{3}$ $= +\ 1\frac{\square}{\square}$ $= +\ \frac{\square}{\square}$

$2\frac{1}{4} + 1\frac{1}{3} =$ _____

4 Tomas painted $1\frac{3}{8}$ walls blue.
He painted $1\frac{5}{10}$ walls white.
How many walls did he paint so far?

_____ walls

☆ **Tell how you solved the problem.**

Assessment

Solve each problem. Show your work.

1 $\frac{1}{5} + \frac{4}{10} =$ _____

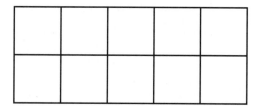

---

2 multiples of 4: ___, ___, ___, ___, ___

multiples of 5: ___, ___, ___, ___, ___   The least common multiple

of 4 and 5 is ___.

$$
\begin{array}{l}
\dfrac{3}{4} \\
+\ \dfrac{2}{5} \\
\hline
\end{array}
=
\begin{array}{l}
\dfrac{3}{4} \times \dfrac{\square}{\square} \\
\dfrac{2}{5} \times \dfrac{\square}{\square}
\end{array}
=
\begin{array}{l}
\dfrac{\square}{\square} \\
+\ \dfrac{\square}{\square} \\
\hline
\end{array}
$$

3
$$
\begin{array}{l}
1\dfrac{5}{6} \\
+\ \dfrac{2}{3} \\
\hline
\end{array}
=
\begin{array}{l}
\dfrac{\square}{\square} \\
\dfrac{2}{3} \times \dfrac{\square}{\square}
\end{array}
=
\begin{array}{l}
\dfrac{\square}{\square} \\
+\ \dfrac{\square}{\square} \\
\hline
\end{array}
$$

$1\frac{5}{6} + \frac{2}{3} =$ _____

---

4 Kayla hiked $1\frac{3}{10}$ miles before lunch.
She hiked $1\frac{4}{5}$ miles after lunch.
About how many miles did she hike?

About _____ miles

⭐ **Tell how you estimated to solve the problem.**

Overview Subtract Fractions

Directions and Sample Answers for Activity Pages

Day 1	See "Model the Skill" below.
Day 2	Tell students that sometimes they will need to find a common multiple of two denominators in order to find the common denominator. Remind students that they find the multiple of a number by multiplying the number by 1, 2, 3, and so on. Help students complete the page. (**1.** 12, 8/12 – 3/12 = 5/12; **2.** 10, 2/2, 5/10 – 4/10 = 1/10; **3.** 9, 18, 27; 6, 12, 18, 24; 18, 3/3, 2/2, 6/18 – 4/18 = 2/18 or 1/9; **4.** 1/6)
Day 3	Read the directions aloud. Tell students that subtracting mixed numbers is like subtracting fractions and that they will need to find a common denominator. Have students write the mixed number as an improper fraction before they subtract. Review how to convert between mixed numbers and improper fractions. Help students complete the page. (**1.** 3/4; **2.** 1 6/9, 15/9, 1 2/9; **3.** 2 3/12 – 1 4/12, 27/12 – 16/12, 11/12; **4.** 1 1/10)
Day 4	Read the directions aloud. You may wish to read the problems aloud also. Help students complete the page, encouraging them to use a drawing to help them understand the problem. (**1.** 1/12; **2.** 6 slices; 6/8 or 3/4 pizza; **3.** 1 1/8 ft; **4.** 1 1/10 ft)
Day 5	Read the directions aloud. Observe as students complete the page. Do students demonstrate how to subtract unlike fractions and mixed numbers? Can they find a common denominator and write an equivalent fraction? Use your observations to plan further instruction and review. (**1.** 3/6 or 1/2; **2.** 5, 10, 15, 20; 2, 4, 6, 8, 10; 10; 2/2, 5/5, 8/10 – 5/10 = 3/10; **3.** 3/4; **4.** 1 1/10)

Model the Skill

◆ Hand out the Day 1 activity page.

◆ **Say:** *Today we are going to subtract fractions.* Write 2/5 – 1/5 on the board. **Ask:** *How do we subtract fractions that have the same denominator?* (Subtract the numerators.) Have students look at problem 1 and note that the denominators are different.

◆ **Ask:** *What is the first thing we need to do to subtract fractions with unlike denominators?* (Use equivalent fractions to write common denominators.) Help students find an equivalent fraction for 1/3 with a denominator of 6. (2/6) Review how to find equivalent fractions.

◆ Help students complete the activity page. Have them use the art to show subtraction by coloring the greater fraction and then crossing out the part being subtracted. You may wish to have students use equivalent fractions to write the sum in simplest form. (**1.** 2/6, 1/6; **2.** 5/8 – 2/8 = 3/8; **3.** 2/6 or 1/3; **4.** 5/10 or 1/2)

Use Manipulatives
Use fraction bars to subtract unlike fractions.
Show equivalent fractions.
Remove the part being subtracted from the greater fraction.

Subtract Fractions

Write an equivalent fraction. Then find the difference.

 1

$$\frac{1}{3} \qquad \frac{\square}{6}$$
$$= $$
$$-\frac{1}{6} \qquad -\frac{1}{6}$$

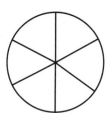

2

$$\frac{5}{8} \qquad \frac{\square}{\square}$$
$$= \qquad \frac{\square}{}$$
$$-\frac{1}{4} \qquad -\frac{}{8}$$

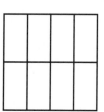

3

$$\frac{1}{2}$$
$$= $$
$$-\frac{1}{6} \qquad -$$

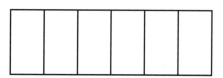

4

$$\frac{3}{5}$$
$$= $$
$$-\frac{1}{10} \qquad -$$

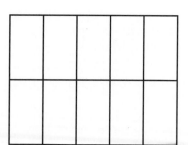

☆ **Tell how you subtract fractions.**

Subtract Fractions

Find a common denominator. Subtract.

1. multiples of 3: 3, 6, 9, 12, 15

   multiples of 4: 4, 8, 12, 16   The least common multiple of 3 and 4 is ___.

$$\begin{array}{c} \frac{2}{3} \\ = \\ -\frac{1}{4} \\ \hline \end{array} \qquad \begin{array}{c} \frac{2}{3} \times \frac{4}{4} \\ \\ \frac{1}{4} \times \frac{3}{3} \end{array} \qquad = \begin{array}{c} \frac{\square}{12} \\ \\ -\frac{\square}{12} \\ \hline \end{array}$$

2. multiples of 2: 2, 4, 6, 8, 10

   multiples of 5: 5, 10, 15   The least common multiple of 5 and 2 is ___.

$$\begin{array}{c} \frac{1}{2} \\ = \\ -\frac{2}{5} \\ \hline \end{array} \qquad \begin{array}{c} \frac{1}{2} \times \frac{5}{5} \\ \\ \frac{2}{5} \times \frac{\square}{\square} \end{array} \qquad = \begin{array}{c} \frac{\square}{\square} \\ \\ -\frac{\square}{\square} \\ \hline \end{array}$$

3. multiples of 9: ___, ___, ___

   multiples of 6: ___, ___, ___, ___   The least common multiple of 9 and 6 is ___.

$$\begin{array}{c} \frac{2}{6} \\ = \\ -\frac{2}{9} \\ \hline \end{array} \qquad \begin{array}{c} \frac{2}{6} \times \frac{\square}{\square} \\ \\ \frac{2}{9} \times \frac{\square}{\square} \end{array} \qquad = \begin{array}{c} \frac{\square}{\square} \\ \\ +\frac{\square}{\square} \\ \hline \end{array}$$

4. $$\begin{array}{c} \frac{1}{2} \\ -\frac{1}{3} \\ \hline \end{array}$$

☆ **Tell how you found the common denominator.**

Subtract Fractions

Find the difference for each problem. Write the difference as a mixed number.

1 $1\frac{1}{2} = 1\frac{2}{4} = \frac{6}{4}$

$\quad\quad -\frac{3}{4} \quad\quad\quad -\frac{3}{4}$
$\quad\quad \overline{} \quad\quad\quad \overline{}$

$1\frac{1}{2} - \frac{3}{4} = $ _____

2 $1\frac{2}{3} = 1\frac{\square}{9} = \frac{\square}{9}$

$\quad\quad -\frac{4}{9} \quad\quad\quad -\frac{4}{9}$
$\quad\quad \overline{} \quad\quad\quad \overline{}$

$1\frac{2}{3} - \frac{4}{9} = $ _____

3 $2\frac{1}{4} \quad\quad 2\frac{\square}{\square} \quad\quad \frac{\square}{\square}$

$\quad -1\frac{1}{3} \quad = \quad 1\frac{\square}{\square} \quad = \quad -\frac{\square}{\square}$
$\quad \overline{}$

$2\frac{1}{4} - 1\frac{1}{3} = $ _____

4 $2\frac{2}{5}$

$\quad -1\frac{3}{10}$
$\quad \overline{}$

$2\frac{2}{5} - 1\frac{3}{10} = $ _____

☆ **Tell how you could estimate the difference.**

Subtract Fractions

Solve each problem. Write the answer in simplest form. Show your work.

1 Maria had $\frac{3}{4}$ liter of milk. She drank $\frac{2}{3}$ of the milk.
How much milk is left?

$$\frac{3}{4} - \frac{2}{3} = \underline{\hspace{2cm}}$$

1 liter

2 A pizza had 8 equal slices. James and his friend
ate $\frac{1}{4}$ of the pizza. How many slices are left?
What fraction of the pizza is left?

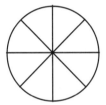

_____

3 Victor saws a board that is $2\frac{1}{2}$ feet long
into two pieces. One piece is $1\frac{3}{8}$ feet
long. How long is the other piece?

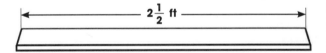

$2\frac{1}{2}$ ft

_____

4 On Monday, $\frac{2}{5}$ of a foot of snow fell.
On Tuesday, $1\frac{1}{2}$ feet of snow fell.
How much more snow fell on Tuesday than Monday?

_____

☆ **Tell how you solved the problem.**

Assessment

Solve each problem. Show your work.

 1

$$\frac{2}{3} - \frac{1}{6} = \underline{\hspace{2cm}}$$

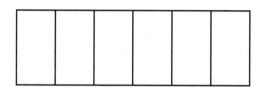

2 multiples of 5: ___, ___, ___, ___

multiples of 2: ___, ___, ___, ___, ___

The least common multiple of 5 and 2 is ___.

$$\begin{array}{c} \frac{4}{5} \\ -\frac{1}{2} \\ \hline \end{array} = \begin{array}{c} \frac{4}{5} \times \frac{\square}{\square} \\ \frac{1}{2} \times \frac{\square}{\square} \end{array} = \begin{array}{c} \frac{\square}{\square} \\ -\frac{\square}{\square} \\ \hline \end{array}$$

3

$$\begin{array}{c} 2\frac{1}{4} \\ -1\frac{1}{2} \\ \hline \end{array}$$

$$2\frac{1}{4} - 1\frac{1}{2} = \underline{\hspace{2cm}}$$

4 Dwayne hiked $2\frac{3}{10}$ miles before lunch.
He hiked $1\frac{1}{5}$ miles after lunch.
How many more miles did he hike before lunch?

_____ miles

☆ **Tell how you solved the problem.**

Overview   Multiply Whole Numbers and Fractions

Directions and Sample Answers for Activity Pages

Day 1	See "Model the Skill" below.
Day 2	Have students look at the art for Problem 1 and discuss how 1/3 x 6 is the same as 6 x 1/3 and how it is different. Then introduce the algorithm, writing the whole number as a fraction and then multiplying numerators and denominators. Have students use art to prove their answers. Help students complete the page. Point out that the order property of multiplication applies to multiplying with fractions. (**1.** 2, 2; **2.** 8/2, 4; **3.** 8/2, 4; **4.** 2)
Day 3	Read the directions aloud. Encourage students to estimate the answer by thinking of the unit fractional part of the whole number and then multiplying by the number of parts ((1/5 x 10) x 2 = 4). Discuss why answers for problems 3–4 are mixed numbers. (**1.** 10/1, 20/5, 4; **2.** 8/1, 24/4, 6; **3.** 7/1, 7/3, 2 1/3; **4.** 11/1, 33/8, 4 1/8)
Day 4	Read the directions aloud. You may wish to read the problems aloud also. Help students complete the page, encouraging them to estimate or to make a drawing to help them understand the problem. (**1.** $9; **2.** 20; **3.** 4; **4.** 6 3/4)
Day 5	Read the directions aloud. Observe as students complete the page. Do students demonstrate how to multiply a unit fraction and a whole number by partitioning? Can they use the standard algorithm? Use your observations to plan further instruction and review. (**1.** 2; **2.** 12/4, 3; **3.** 10/1, 20/3, 6 2/3; **4.** 9 3/5)

Model the Skill

◆ Hand out the Day 1 activity page and twelve counters to each student.

◆ **Say:** *Today we are going to multiply a fraction and a whole number.* **Ask:** *When we multiply two whole numbers, like 3 x 6, will the product be more or less than 6?* (more) *If we multiply 6 by a fraction, will the product be more or less than 6?* (less) *Why?* Help students understand that when multiplying by a fraction, they are finding a part of the whole number.

◆ Have students look at problem 1 and explain what the art shows. **Ask:** *Why does 1/3 of 6 equal 2?* Build the idea of partitioning (dividing) into equal groups as a way to understand multiplying by a fraction.

◆ Help students complete the activity page. Have students use counters to duplicate the art shown for each problem and then model the multiplication by partitioning. (**2.** 3; **3.** 3; **4.** 5)

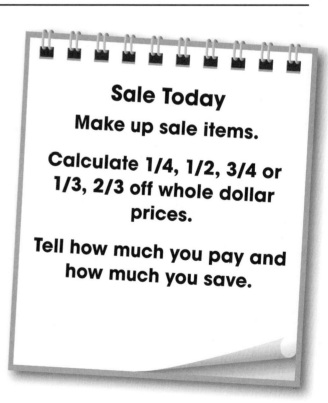

Sale Today
Make up sale items.

Calculate 1/4, 1/2, 3/4 or 1/3, 2/3 off whole dollar prices.

Tell how much you pay and how much you save.

Multiply Whole Numbers and Fractions

Find a fraction of a whole number.

1 $\frac{1}{3}$ of 6

$\frac{1}{3}$ x 6 = _____

2 $\frac{1}{2}$ of 6

$\frac{1}{2}$ x 6 = _____

3 $\frac{1}{4}$ of 12

$\frac{1}{4}$ x 12 = _____

4 $\frac{1}{2}$ of 10

$\frac{1}{2}$ x 10 = _____

⭐ **Tell how you know the product will be less than 10.**

Multiply Whole Numbers and Fractions

Multiply. Write each product as a whole number.

1

$\frac{1}{3}$ x 6 = _____

1/3 of a set of 6

$6 \times \frac{1}{3}$ = _____

6 sets of $\frac{1}{3}$

2

$\frac{1}{2}$ x 8

$\frac{1}{2} \times \frac{8}{1} = \frac{\square}{\square}$ = _____

3

$8 \times \frac{1}{2}$

$\frac{8}{1} \times \frac{1}{2} = \frac{\square}{\square}$ = _____

   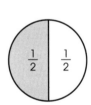

4

$\frac{1}{6}$ x 12

$12 \times \frac{1}{6}$ = _____

 **Tell why the product is the same.**

Multiply Whole Numbers and Fractions

Multiply. Write the answer in simplest form.

 1

$\dfrac{2}{5} \times 10$

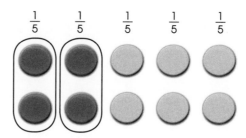

$\dfrac{2}{5} \times \dfrac{10}{\square} = \dfrac{\square}{\square} =$ _____

 2

$\dfrac{3}{4} \times 8$

$\dfrac{3}{4} \times \dfrac{8}{\square} = \dfrac{\square}{\square} =$ _____

3

$\dfrac{1}{3} \times 7$

$\dfrac{1}{3} \times \dfrac{7}{\square} = \dfrac{\square}{\square} =$ _____

4

$\dfrac{3}{8} \times 11$

$\dfrac{3}{8} \times \dfrac{11}{\square} = \dfrac{\square}{\square} =$ _____

 Tell how you found the product.

Multiply Whole Numbers and Fractions

Solve each problem. Write the answer in simplest form. Show your work.

1 A toy that costs $27 is on sale for $\frac{1}{3}$ less.
How much money will you save if you
buy the toy on sale?

$\frac{1}{3}$ x 27 = _____

2 A baker made 32 loaves of bread.
He sold $\frac{5}{8}$ of the loaves. How many
loaves did he sell?

$\frac{5}{8}$ x 32 = _____

3 A bike shop has 16 bikes on display.
One-fourth of the bikes are red.
How many bikes are red?

_____ bikes

4 A piece of ribbon is 9 inches long.
Kayla uses $\frac{3}{4}$ of the ribbon for a project.
How many inches of ribbon did she use?

_____ inches

☆ **Tell how you solved the problem.**

Assessment

Solve each problem. Show your work.

1

$\frac{1}{8}$ of 16

$\frac{1}{8}$ × 16 = _____

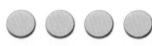

2

12 × $\frac{1}{4}$

$\frac{12}{1}$ × $\frac{1}{4}$ = $\frac{\square}{\square}$ = _____

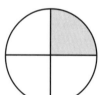
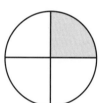
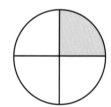

3

$\frac{2}{3}$ × 10

$\frac{2}{3}$ × $\frac{10}{\square}$ = $\frac{\square}{\square}$ = _____

4 Ms. Ortiz bought a 12-kilogram bag of dog food.
Her dog ate $\frac{4}{5}$ of the food in a month.
How many kilograms of food did the dog eat in a month?

_____ kilograms

☆ **Tell how you solved the problem.**

Overview   Multiply Fractions

Directions and Sample Answers for Activity Pages

Day 1	See "Model the Skill" below.
Day 2	Have students look at the art for problem 1 and discuss how 2/3 x 1/2 is the same as 1/2 x 2/3 and how it is different. Encourage students to use the algorithm for multiplying fractions, and have them color the art to show the multiplication. Help students complete the page. Point out that the order property of multiplication applies. (**1.** 2/6; **2.** 5/16; **3.** 4/20 or 1/5; **4.** 3/8)
Day 3	Read the directions aloud. Review how to simplify a fraction by dividing the numerator and denominator by their greatest common factor. Tell students they may also simplify a fraction before multiplying. (**1.** 4/12, 1/3; **2.** 18/32, 9/16; **3.** 10/18, 5/9; **4.** 8/40, 1/5)
Day 4	Read the directions aloud. You may wish to read the problems aloud also. Help students complete the page, encouraging them to make a drawing to help them understand the problem. (**1.** 2/15; **2.** 1/8; **3.** 1/2; **4.** 3/8)
Day 5	Read the directions aloud. Observe as students complete the page. Do students demonstrate how to multiply two fractions using a model or an equation? Can they use the standard algorithm? Use your observations to plan further instruction and review. (**1.** 1/8; **2.** 3/16; **3.** 1/5; **4.** 1/5)

Model the Skill

◆ Hand out the Day 1 activity page.

◆ **Say:** *Today we are going to multiply two fractions. Remember, when we multiplied two whole numbers, the product was greater than each factor. When we multiply two fractions, like 1/3 x 1/2, will the product be greater or less than each factor?* (less) *Why?* Help students understand that when multiplying two fractions, they are finding a fraction of a part.

◆ Have students look at problem 1 and explain what the art shows. **Ask:** *Why is the product 1/6?* Have students identify 1/2 of the whole and 1/3 of the whole. Then have them point to the section that represents 1/3 of 1/2.

◆ Help students complete the activity page. You may wish to have students color the art shown for each problem using a different color for each factor. (**2.** 1/8; **3.** 1/12; **4.** 1/10)

Use Manipulatives
Multiply 1/2 by 1/4.

Fold a paper square in half horizontally and color 1/2.

Fold the square vertically into fourths.

Use a different color to show 1/4 of the square.

The part with both colors is the product.

Continue in the same way with other squares, finding 2/4, 3/4, 1/3, and 2/3 of 1/2.

Multiply Fractions

Find a fraction of a part.

 1

$\frac{1}{3}$ of $\frac{1}{2}$

$\frac{1}{3}$ x $\frac{1}{2}$ = _____

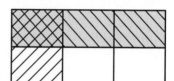

2

$\frac{1}{2}$ of $\frac{1}{4}$

$\frac{1}{2}$ x $\frac{1}{4}$ = _____

3

$\frac{1}{4}$ of $\frac{1}{3}$

$\frac{1}{4}$ x $\frac{1}{3}$ = _____

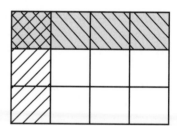

4

$\frac{1}{5}$ of $\frac{1}{2}$

$\frac{1}{5}$ x $\frac{1}{2}$ = _____

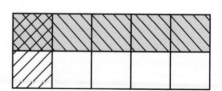

☆ **Tell how you know the product will be less than one-half.**

Multiply Fractions

Multiply. Show your work.

 1

$\frac{2}{3}$ x $\frac{1}{2}$ = _____

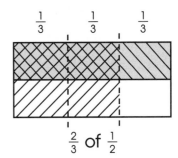

$\frac{1}{2}$ shaded $\frac{2}{3}$ of $\frac{1}{2}$

$\frac{1}{2}$ x $\frac{2}{3}$ = _____

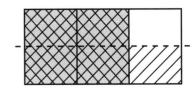

$\frac{2}{3}$ shaded

 2

$\frac{5}{8}$ x $\frac{1}{2}$ = _____

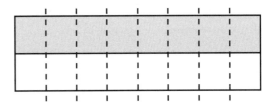

3

$\frac{1}{4}$ x $\frac{4}{5}$ = _____

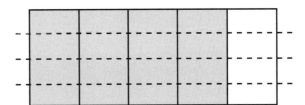

4

$\frac{3}{4}$ x $\frac{1}{2}$ = _____

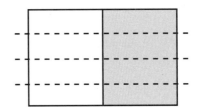

 Tell how you multiplied the fractions.

Multiply Fractions

Multiply. Write the answer in simplest form.

$\dfrac{2}{3} \times \dfrac{2}{4} = \dfrac{\square}{\square} =$ _____

$\dfrac{6}{8} \times \dfrac{3}{4} = \dfrac{\square}{\square} =$ _____

③

$\dfrac{5}{6} \times \dfrac{2}{3} = \dfrac{\square}{\square} =$ _____

④

$\dfrac{2}{5} \times \dfrac{4}{8} = \dfrac{\square}{\square} =$ _____

 Tell how you found the simplest form of the product.

Multiply Fractions

Solve each problem. Write the answer in simplest form. Show your work.

① Two-thirds of a pan of corn bread is left.
Marc eats $\frac{1}{5}$ of what is left. How much
of the pan of corn bread did Marc eat?

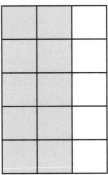

$\frac{1}{5} \times \frac{2}{3} =$ _____

② In a bakery, $\frac{1}{2}$ of the cupcakes are chocolate.
Only $\frac{1}{4}$ of the chocolate cupcakes have sprinkles on top.
What fraction of all the cupcakes are chocolate with sprinkles?

$\frac{1}{2} \times \frac{1}{4} =$ _____

③ Martin painted $\frac{3}{4}$ of a wall with primer.
Then he painted $\frac{4}{6}$ of the wall blue.
What fraction of the wall did he paint twice?

_____ of the wall

④ Beth has $\frac{6}{8}$ kilogram of cheese.
She used half of that amount to make sandwiches.
What fraction of a kilogram did she use?

_____ kilogram

⭐ **Tell how you solved the problem.**

Assessment

Solve each problem. Show your work.

$\frac{1}{4}$ of $\frac{1}{2}$

$\frac{1}{4}$ x $\frac{1}{2}$ = _____

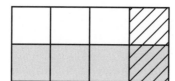 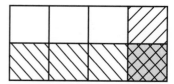

---

② $\frac{1}{2}$ x $\frac{3}{8}$ = _____

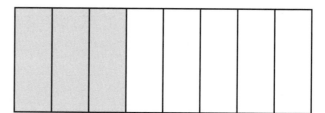

---

③ $\frac{2}{8}$ x $\frac{4}{5}$ = _____

---

④ Elena had $\frac{2}{3}$ kilogram of cat food.
Her cat ate $\frac{3}{10}$ of the food yesterday.
What fraction of a kilogram of food did her cat eat?

_____ kilogram

☆ **Tell how you solved the problem.**

Overview   Multiply Mixed Numbers

Directions and Sample Answers for Activity Pages

Day 1	See "Model the Skill" below.
Day 2	Have students look at the art for problem 1 and discuss how the art shows multiplication of 2 3/4 x 2/3. Remind students that the order property of multiplication applies to fractions. Review how to write a fraction in simplest form by dividing the numerator and denominator by their greatest common factor. Encourage students to use the algorithm for multiplying fractions. (**1.** 11/4, 1 5/6; **2.** 8/5, 1 1/3; **3.** 14/4, 1 5/16; **4.** 12/5, 1 5/7)
Day 3	Point out that an area model can be used to show multiplication of mixed numbers. Have students use the art, counting whole and part squares to find the area of a rectangle 3 1/2 x 2 1/2 units. (8 whole squares + 1/2 and 1/4 square) Note that the product is in square units. Hand out large grid paper so students may draw a model for problems 2–4. (**1.** 7/2 x 5/2 = 8 3/4; **2.** 3/2 x 8/3 = 4; **3.** 5/2 x 7/5 = 3 1/2; **4.** 11/4 x 9/2 = 12 3/8)
Day 4	Read the directions aloud. You may wish to read the problems aloud also. Help students complete the page, encouraging them to use the drawing to help them understand the problem. (**1.** 1 1/4; **2.** 2 1/5; **3.** 16 1/2; **4.** 11 1/9)
Day 5	Read the directions aloud. Observe as students complete the page. Do students demonstrate how to multiply mixed numbers using a model or an equation? Can they accurately find and simplify improper fractions? Use your observations to plan further instruction and review. (**1.** 9/16; **2.** 8/9; **3.** 3/2 x 5/2 = 3 3/4 square units; **4.** 3)

Model the Skill

◆ Hand out the Day 1 activity page.

◆ **Say:** *Today we are going to multiply mixed numbers. We multiply mixed numbers the same way we multiply fractions. Look at problem 1. How can we write 1 1/2 as a fraction?* (2/2 + 1/2 = 3/2) Have students use the art to explain the improper fraction.

◆ **Say:** *Now we are going to take 1/4 of 3 halves, so we cut 1 1/2 into fourths.* Have students look at the art. **Ask:** *How many fourths should we mark with an X?* (1/4 of each rectangle) Have them count the number of parts in one whole rectangle. (8) The part that is both shaded and has an X is the product. Connect the algorithm to the art. (1/4 x 3/2 = 3/8)

◆ Help students complete the activity page. You may wish to have students draw rectangles to represent problems 3 and 4. (**2.** 5/2, 5/16; **3.** 8/3, 8/15; **4.** 7/4, 7/12)

Use Manipulatives

Use grid paper to create area models.

Draw a rectangle to show multiplication of mixed numbers, such as 4 1/2 x 2 3/4.

Determine area by counting square units, including parts, and by multiplying length and width.

Multiply Mixed Numbers

Write a mixed number as an improper fraction. Then multiply.

1 $\frac{1}{4} \times 1\frac{1}{2}$

$1\frac{1}{2} = \frac{\square}{2}$

$1\frac{1}{2}$ or $\frac{3}{2}$ shaded

$\frac{1}{4} \times \frac{\square}{2} =$ _____

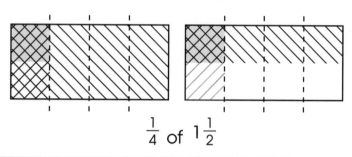

$\frac{1}{4}$ of $1\frac{1}{2}$

---

2 $\frac{1}{8} \times 2\frac{1}{2}$

$2\frac{1}{2} = \frac{\square}{2}$

$\frac{1}{8} \times \frac{\square}{2} =$ _____

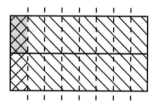 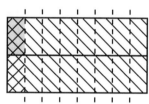 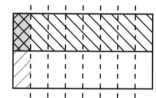

---

3 $2\frac{2}{3} \times \frac{1}{5}$

$2\frac{2}{3} = \frac{\square}{3}$

$\frac{\square}{3} \times \frac{1}{5} =$ _____

---

4 $\frac{1}{3} \times 1\frac{3}{4}$

$1\frac{3}{4} = \frac{\square}{4}$

$\frac{1}{3} \times \frac{\square}{4} =$ _____

☆ **Tell how you write a mixed number as an improper fraction.**

Multiply Mixed Numbers

Multiply. Write the answer in simplest form.

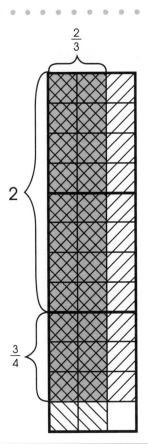

$2\frac{3}{4} \times \frac{2}{3}$

$2\frac{3}{4} = \frac{\square}{4}$

$\frac{\square}{4} \times \frac{2}{3} = $ _____

---

2 $1\frac{3}{5} \times \frac{5}{6}$

$1\frac{3}{5} = \frac{\square}{5}$

$\frac{\square}{5} \times \frac{5}{6} = $ _____

---

3 $\frac{3}{8} \times 3\frac{2}{4}$

$3\frac{2}{4} = \frac{\square}{4}$

$\frac{3}{8} \times \frac{\square}{4} = $ _____

---

4 $\frac{5}{7} \times 2\frac{2}{5}$

$2\frac{2}{5} = \frac{\square}{5}$

$\frac{5}{7} \times \frac{\square}{5} = $ _____

 Tell how you find the simplest form of a fraction.

Multiply Mixed Numbers

Multiply. Write the answer in simplest form.

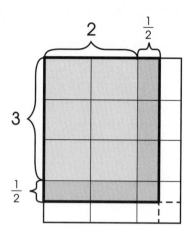

$3\frac{1}{2} \times 2\frac{1}{2}$

$3\frac{1}{2} = \dfrac{\square}{2}$ $2\frac{1}{2} = \dfrac{\square}{2}$

$\dfrac{\square}{2} \times \dfrac{\square}{2} =$ _____

---

2 $1\frac{1}{2} \times 2\frac{2}{3}$

$1\frac{1}{2} = \dfrac{\square}{2}$ $2\frac{2}{3} = \dfrac{\square}{3}$

$\dfrac{\square}{2} \times \dfrac{\square}{3} =$ _____

---

3 $2\frac{1}{2} \times 2\frac{2}{5}$

$2\frac{1}{2} = \dfrac{\square}{2}$ $1\frac{2}{5} = \dfrac{\square}{5}$

$\dfrac{\square}{2} \times \dfrac{\square}{5} =$ _____

---

4 $2\frac{3}{4} \times 4\frac{1}{2}$

$2\frac{3}{4} = \dfrac{\square}{4}$ $4\frac{1}{2} = \dfrac{\square}{2}$

$\dfrac{\square}{4} \times \dfrac{\square}{2} =$ _____

☆ **Tell how you multiply mixed numbers.**

Multiply Mixed Numbers

Solve each problem. Write the answer in simplest form. Show your work.

1 One and two-thirds pans of macaroni are left.
Steve and his brothers eat $\frac{3}{4}$ of what is left.
How much of the pans of macaroni did they eat?

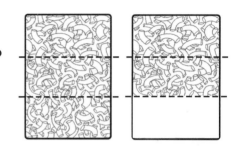

$\frac{3}{4}$ x $1\frac{2}{3}$ = _____

2 Mrs. Myer bought $5\frac{1}{2}$ pounds of apples. She used $\frac{2}{5}$
of that amount to make fruit salad. How many pounds
of apples did she use for the fruit salad?

_____ pounds

3 Jasmine's garden is $4\frac{1}{2}$ meters long and $3\frac{2}{3}$
meters wide. What is the area of her garden?

_____ square meters

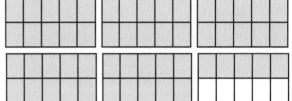

4 A square rug is $3\frac{1}{3}$ feet long.
How many square feet will the rug cover?

_____ square feet

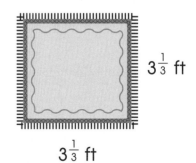

$3\frac{1}{3}$ ft

 Tell how you solved the problem.

Assessment

Solve each problem. Show your work.

1 $\frac{1}{2} \times 1\frac{1}{8}$

$1\frac{1}{8} = \dfrac{\square}{8}$

$\dfrac{1}{2} \times \dfrac{\square}{8} = $ _____

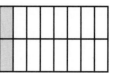

2 $1\frac{2}{6} \times \frac{2}{3}$

$1\frac{2}{6} = \dfrac{\square}{6}$

$\dfrac{\square}{6} \times \dfrac{2}{3} = $ _____

3 $1\frac{1}{2} \times 2\frac{1}{2}$

$1\frac{1}{2} = \dfrac{\square}{2}$ $2\frac{1}{2} = \dfrac{\square}{2}$

$\dfrac{\square}{2} \times \dfrac{\square}{2} = $ _____

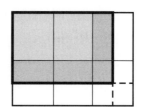

4   A rectangular gym mat is $2\frac{2}{5}$ meters long and $1\frac{1}{4}$ meters wide. What is the area of the gym mat?

_____ square meters

⭐ **Tell how you solved the problem.**

Overview   Divide Whole Numbers and Fractions

Directions and Sample Answers for Activity Pages

Day 1	See "Model the Skill" below.
Day 2	Tell students that today they are going to divide a fraction by a whole number. Discuss whether the quotient will be greater or less than the fraction they are dividing. Use the art to help students see that they will get a smaller part. Day 2 problems use the same numbers as Day 1. Have students compare to reinforce what dividing by a fraction or a whole number means. (**1.** 1/6; **2.** 1/12; **3.** 1/6; **4.** 1/10)
Day 3	Read the directions aloud. Emphasize that the fraction bar means division, so the fraction 2/5 means 2 divided by 5. Review how to do long division and why the quotient can be a mixed number. Have students check their answers by multiplying. (**1.** 2/5; **2.** 6/4 or 1 1/2; **3.** 6 1/4; **4.** 3 3/5)
Day 4	Read the directions aloud. You may wish to read the problems aloud also. Help students complete the page, encouraging them to use or make a drawing to help them understand the problem. Make the connection with finding area of a rectangle in problem 4. (**1.** 2/3; **2.** 20; **3.** 1/8; **4.** 6 1/4)
Day 5	Read the directions aloud. Observe as students complete the page. Do students demonstrate how to divide a fraction by a whole number? A whole number by a fraction? Can they show their work using a model or an equation? Use your observations to plan further instruction and review. (**1.** 20; **2.** 1/16; **3.** 5/6; **4.** 1/10)

Model the Skill

◆ Hand out the Day 1 activity page.

◆ **Say:** *Today we are going to divide a whole number by a fraction. Do you think if I divide a whole number like 3 by a fraction I will have more than 3 pieces or less than 3 pieces?* (more) Have students look at problem 1.

◆ **Ask:** *How many circles do you see? How many halves do you see?* (6) *So 3 divided by 1/2 is equal to 6. Do you agree?* Encourage students to discuss why the quotient is 6, using the art to support their understanding.

◆ Help students complete the activity page. You may wish to have students draw a picture to represent problems 3 and 4. (**2.** 12; **3.** 6; **4.** 10)

Division Game

**Make a set of cards:
1/2, 1/3, 1/4, 1/5, and 2–5.**

Deal two fraction cards and two whole number cards to each player.

Players take turns dividing the numbers on two of their cards and recording the quotient as their score.

Play for highest score. Then play for lowest score.

Divide Whole Numbers and Fractions

Find the quotient for each problem.

$3 \div \dfrac{1}{2} =$ _____

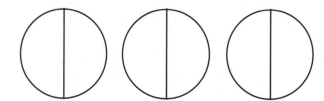

$3 \div \dfrac{1}{4} =$ _____

3

$2 \div \dfrac{1}{3} =$ _____

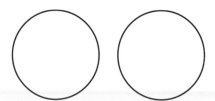

4

$5 \div \dfrac{1}{2} =$ _____

⭐ **Tell how you know the quotient will be more than 5.**

Divide Whole Numbers and Fractions

Find the quotient for each problem.

 1

$\frac{1}{2} \div 3 =$ _____

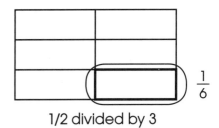

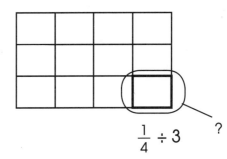

1/2 divided by 3

2

$\frac{1}{4} \div 3 =$ _____

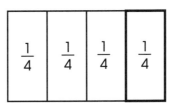

$\frac{1}{4} \div 3$?

3

$\frac{1}{3} \div 2 =$ _____

4

$\frac{1}{5} \div 2 =$ _____

⭐ **Tell how you know the quotient will be less than 1/5.**

Divide Whole Numbers and Fractions

Divide. If there is a remainder, write it as a fraction.

1 $2 \div 5 =$ _____

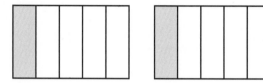

2 $6 \div 4 =$ _____

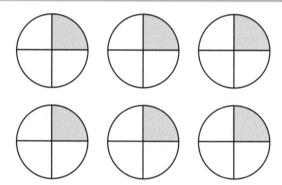

3 $25 \div 4 =$ _____

$$4\overline{)25}$$

4 $18 \div 5 =$ _____

$$5\overline{)18}$$

☆ **Tell how you know the remainder will be less than $\frac{5}{5}$.**

Name _____

Divide Whole Numbers and Fractions

Solve each problem. Show your work.

① Three friends share 2 apples equally.
What part of an apple does each friend get?

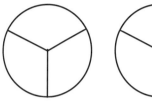

$2 \div 3 =$ _____

② Steve bought 10 cans of cat food.
His cat eats 1/2 can each day.
How many days will it take the cat
to eat all the food?

$10 \div \frac{1}{2} =$ _____

③ One-half of a pizza pie is left. Kayla wants to
cut it into 4 equal pieces. What part of the
pizza pie will each piece be?

$\frac{1}{2} \div 4 =$ _____

④ A rug has an area of 25 square feet.
The width of the rug is 4 feet. How long is the rug?

$25 \div 4 =$ _____ feet

☆ **Tell how you can check that your answer is correct.**

Assessment

Solve each problem. Show your work.

 1

$4 \div \dfrac{1}{5}$ = _____

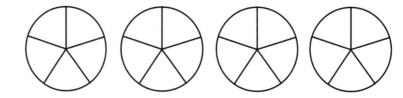

2

$\dfrac{1}{4} \div 4$ = _____

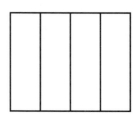

3

$5 \div 6$ = _____

---

4   Dan read 1/2 of the book in 5 days.
    What part of the whole book did he read each day?

    _____ of the book

☆ **Tell how you solved the problem.**

Overview Convert Among Metric Units

Directions and Sample Answers for Activity Pages

Day 1	See "Model the Skill" below.
Day 2	Discuss what the chart shows. Be sure students understand the relative size of the units and note the abbreviations used. You may wish to include milligram (mg). Help students complete the page. Remind students that they can multiply to check their division. (**1.** 0.002; **2.** 0.013, 13 ÷ 1,000 = 0.013; **3.** 5,000, 5 x 1,000 = 5,000; **4.** 0.009 t)
Day 3	Read the directions aloud. Be sure students understand the relative size of the units and note the abbreviations used. Help students complete the page. (**1.** 0.002; **2.** 1.5, 1,500 ÷ 1,000 = 1.5; **3.** 4,000, 4 x 1,000 = 4,000; **4.** 0.028)
Day 4	Read the directions aloud. You may also wish to read the word problems aloud. Tell students they may look back at the equivalents between units if they do not remember them. (**1.** 0.65; **2.** 2,000; **3.** 250 mL, 0.25 L; **4.** 0.15 m)
Day 5	Read the directions aloud. Observe as students complete the page. Can students convert among units of measurement? Can they use conversions to solve problems? Use your observations to plan further instruction and review. (**1.** 1.7, 17 ÷ 10 = 1.7; **2.** 3,000; **3.** 1.4; **4.** 0.4)

Model the Skill

◆ Hand out the Day 1 activity page.

◆ **Ask:** *What are some units of length in the metric system?* Write the units and their abbreviations on the board (km, m, cm, mm). You may wish to include decameter (dm). Allow students to examine a cm ruler and discuss that a millimeter is 1/10 of a centimeter and relate it to decimal notation. Be sure students understand the relative size of all the units of length.

◆ **Say:** *When we operate with units of length, we need to work with the same units, so sometimes we need to convert a smaller unit to a larger unit, or a larger unit to a smaller unit. Look at the chart on the side of the page.*

◆ **Ask:** *What do you notice? How can we convert a meter into centimeters?* (multiply by 100) *How can we convert a centimeter into a meter?* (divide by 100) Help students understand that when we multiply to convert from a larger unit to a smaller unit, we will get more smaller units. Conversely, when we divide, we will get fewer (or a part of) large units.

◆ Continue in the same manner, converting among units. Help students complete the activity page. (**1.** 0.03; **2.** 0.5, 5 ÷ 10 = 0.5; **3.** 2,000; **4.** 0.015)

Team Game

Teacher gives a measurement in cm, m, g, or mL.

Teams convert the measurement to a larger unit and vie to shout it out first.

Teacher records a correct conversion under the team's name.

Calculators may be used.

Convert Among Metric Units

Complete each problem. Use the chart to help you.

1   3 centimeters (cm) = _____ meter (m)

Divide: 3 ÷ 100 = _____

---

2   5 millimeters (mm) = _____ centimeter

Divide: _____ ÷ _____ = _____

---

3   2 kilometers (km) = _____ meters

Multiply: 2 x 1,000 = _____

---

4   15 m = _____ km

Metric Units of Length
x 1,000
1 km = 1000 m
1 m = 0.001 km
÷ 1,000
x 100
1 m = 100 cm
1 cm = 0.01 m
÷ 100
x 10
1 cm = 10 mm
1 mm = 0.1 cm
÷ 10

☆ **Tell how you can convert meters to kilometers.**

Name _____

Convert Among Metric Units

Complete each problem. Use the chart to help you.

1 2 kilograms (kg) = _____ metric ton (t)

Divide: 2 ÷ 1,000 = _____

Metric Units of Mass
x 1,000
1 t = 1000 kg
1 kg = 0.001 t
÷ 1,000
x 1,000
1 kg = 1000 g
1 g = 0.001 kg
÷ 1,000

2 13 grams (g) = _____ kilogram

Divide: _____ ÷ _____ = _____

3 5 kilograms = _____ grams

Multiply: _____ x _____ = _____

4 9 kg = _____ t

☆ **Tell how you know your answer is correct.**

Convert Among Metric Units

Complete each problem. Use the chart to help you.

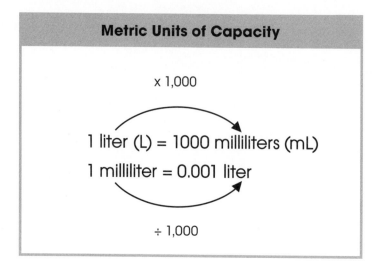

Metric Units of Capacity

x 1,000

1 liter (L) = 1000 milliliters (mL)

1 milliliter = 0.001 liter

÷ 1,000

1   2 mL = _____ L

     Divide: 2 ÷ 1,000 = _____

2   1,500 mL = _____ L

     Divide: _____ ÷ _____ = _____

3   4 L = _____ mL

     Multiply: _____ x _____ = _____

4   28 mL = _____ L

☆ **Tell what to do when you want to convert from a smaller unit to a larger unit.**

Convert Among Metric Units

Solve each problem. Show your work.

1   Shawn lives 650 meters away from school.
    What is the distance in kilometers?

    650 m = _____ km

2   An elephant has a mass of 2 metric tons.
    How many kilograms is that?

    2 t = _____ kg

3   A recipe calls for 750 milliliters of milk.
    Amanda has 1 liter of milk. How much milk
    will be left after Amanda makes the recipe?

    _____ milliliters or _____ liter

4   Jack finished the race 35 centimeters ahead
    of Don and 0.5 meter ahead of Paul. How many
    meters were there between Don and Paul?

    _____ m

☆ **Tell how you solved the problem.**

Assessment

Solve each problem. Show your work.

1 17 millimeters = _____ centimeters

2 3 liters = _____ milliliters

3 David makes a fruit salad using 625 grams of
peaches, 375 grams of strawberries, and 0.4 kilogram
of grapes. How many kilograms of fruit salad did he make?

_____ kg

4 It is a 2-kilometer hike to the waterfall. Anna runs for
300 meters and then walks for 1,300 meters. How many
more kilometers must Anna hike to reach the waterfall?

_____ km

⭐ **Tell how you solved the problem.**

_____

_____

Overview Convert Among Customary Units

Directions and Sample Answers for Activity Pages

Day 1	See "Model the Skill" below.
Day 2	Discuss equivalents among customary units of weight. Be sure students understand the relative size of the units and note the abbreviations used. Note that ton (T) is not the same as metric ton (t). Review how to multiply fractions for problem 3. For problem 4, students should realize that they multiply 5 x 16 and then add 6. (**1.** 3; **2.** 2, 32 ÷ 16 = 2; **3.** 3,000, 3/2 x 2,000/1 = 6,000/2 = 3,000; **4.** 86)
Day 3	Read the directions aloud. Be sure students understand the relative size of the units and note the abbreviations used. Tell students that when ounces are used to measure how much something holds, they are called fluid ounces, which are different from the ounces that tell weight. Help students complete the page. (**1.** 6; **2.** 6, 24 ÷ 4 = 6; **3.** 10, 5 x 2 = 10; **4.** 4)
Day 4	Read the directions aloud. You may also wish to read the word problems aloud. Tell students they may look back at the equivalents between units if they do not remember them. (**1.** 32; **2.** 3; **3.** 4 lb 8 oz, 4 1/2; **4.** 1 1/4)
Day 5	Read the directions aloud. Observe as students complete the page. Can students convert among units of measurement? Can they use conversions to solve problems? Use your observations to plan further instruction and review. (**1.** 8, 16,000 ÷ 2,000 = 8; **2.** 13 1/3, 13 yd 1 ft; **3.** 1 3/4 qt; **4.** 114)

Model the Skill

◆ Hand out the Day 1 activity page.

◆ **Ask:** *What are some units of length in the customary system?* Write the units and their abbreviations on the board (in., ft, yd, mi). Be sure students understand the relative size of all the units of length.

◆ **Say:** *When we operate with units of length in the customary system, we often mix units, like 5 feet 6 inches, or we use fractions, like 5 1/2 feet.* Have students look at the chart on the page and discuss equivalents. Note that they are not powers of ten like in the metric system.

◆ **Ask:** *When we need to convert a smaller unit to a larger unit, what do you think we do?* (divide) *How many feet is 60 inches?* (5 ft) *What did you use as the divisor?* (12) *When we need to convert a larger unit to a smaller unit, what do you think we do?* (multiply) *How many feet is 4 yards?* (12 ft) *What did you use as the multiplier?* (3) (**1.** 4; **2.** 18, 54 ÷ 3 = 18; **3.** 72, 2 x 36 = 72; **4.** 10 1/3, 10 yd 1 ft.)

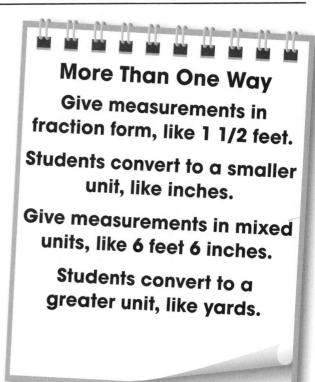

More Than One Way

Give measurements in fraction form, like 1 1/2 feet.
Students convert to a smaller unit, like inches.

Give measurements in mixed units, like 6 feet 6 inches.
Students convert to a greater unit, like yards.

Convert Among Customary Units

Complete each problem.

Customary Units of Length	
12 inches (in.) = 1 foot (ft)	36 inches = 1 yard
3 feet = 1 yard (yd)	5,280 feet = 1 mile (mi)

1 48 inches = ___4___ feet

   Divide: 48 ÷ 12 = ___4___

   > 12 in. = 1 ft

2 54 feet = ___18___ yards

   Divide: ___3___ ÷ ___54___ = ___18___

   > 3 ft = 1 yd

   $$3\overline{)54}$$
   1 yd
   3
   24

3 2 yd = ___102___ in.

   Multiply: 2 x ___36___ = ___102___

   > 1 yd = 36 in.

   36
   +36
   102

4 31 ft = ___10___ yd

   31 ft = ___10___ yd ___1___ ft

   > ___3___ ft = 1 yd

⭐ **Tell how you can convert feet to yards.**

Convert Among Customary Units

Complete each problem.

Customary Units of Weight
16 ounces (oz) = 1 pound (lb)
2,000 pounds = 1 ton (T)

1   6,000 pounds = __3__ tons

> 2,000 lb = 1 T

Divide: 6,000 ÷ 2,000 = __3__

---

2   32 ounces = __2__ pounds

> 16 oz = 1 lb

Divide: __32__ ÷ __16__ = __2__

---

3 $1\frac{1}{2}$ tons = __3,000__ pounds

> 1 T = 2,000 lb

$1\frac{1}{2} = \frac{3}{2}$

Multiply: $\frac{3}{2}$ x __3,000__ = __3,000__

---

4   5 pounds 6 ounces = __186__ ounces

> 1 lb = __16__ oz

$$\begin{array}{r} 3\ 1\ 6 \\ 5\ \overline{}\ \frac{5}{8\ 0} \end{array}$$

⭐ **Tell how you know your answer is correct.**

Convert Among Customary Units

Complete each problem.

Customary Units of Capacity
8 fluid ounces (fl oz) = 1 cup (c)   2 pints = 1 quart (qt) 2 cups = 1 pint (pt)   4 quarts = 1 gallon (gal)

1 48 fluid ounces = _____ cups

> 8 fl oz. = 1 c

Divide: 48 ÷ 8 = _____

2 24 quarts = _____ gallons

> 4 qt = 1 gal

Divide: _____ ÷ _____ = _____

3 5 pints = _____ cups

> 1 pt = 2 c

Multiply: _____ x _____ = _____

4 16 cups = _____ quarts

> ____ c = 1 qt

☆ **Tell what to do when you want to convert from a smaller unit to a larger unit.**

Convert Among Customary Units

Solve each problem. Draw a picture to help you. Show your work.

1. Yuji wants to put two boxes on a shelf. One box
    is 14 inches long. The other box is $1\frac{1}{2}$ feet long.
    How long are the boxes altogether?

    _____ inches

2. A water bottle holds 24 fluid ounces.
    How many cups of water is that?

    24 fl oz = _____ cups

3. Amy buys 40 ounces of rice and 32 ounces of beans.
    How many pounds of rice and beans did she buy?

    _____ lb _____ oz or _____ pounds

4. A recipe calls for 3 cups of milk. Amanda has $\frac{1}{2}$ gallon
    of milk. How much milk will be left after Amanda makes the recipe?

    _____ quarts

★ **Tell how you solved the problem.**

Assessment

Solve each problem. Show your work.

1   16,000 pounds = _____ tons

_____ ÷ _____ = _____

---

2   40 ft = _____ yd

40 ft = _____ yd _____ ft

---

3   Mia bought seven drink boxes for a trip. Each box holds
8 fluid ounces of juice. How many quarts of juice is that?

_____ qt

---

4   Deepak is building a skateboard ramp. He puts a
board $3\frac{1}{2}$ feet long end-to-end with a board that is
2 yards long. How many inches long are the boards together?

_____ inches

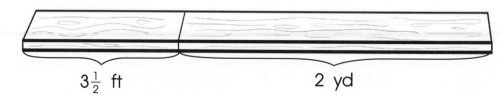

$3\frac{1}{2}$ ft   2 yd

☆ **Tell how you solved the problem.**

Overview   Use Measurement Data

Directions and Sample Answers for Activity Pages

Day 1	See "Model the Skill" below.
Day 2	Discuss the shape of the data, where it clusters and where there are gaps. Help students understand the meaning of greatest and least value, data set, range, and median. Be sure students understand that median is the middle value of 11 data points listed in order from least to greatest. (**1.** Answers will vary. **2.** 7 1/2, 5; **3.** 2 1/2; **4.** 5 1/2)
Day 3	Read the directions aloud. Help students complete the page. Help students find the average for problem 4. Have students combine Xs to make equal amounts. Then show them how to add the values of the data set and divide by the number of points in the set. (**1.** Answers will vary. **2.** 6; **3.** 1 1/2 fl oz; **4.** 1)
Day 4	Read the directions aloud. Help students display data from the frequency table in a line plot. Discuss how to answer the questions and whether the mode or the average (problems 2–3) is the more useful information. (Check students' line plots. **1.** 9; **2.** 1/2 lb; **3.** 1 lb)
Day 5	Read the directions aloud. Observe as students complete the page. Can students display given data in a line plot? Can they use information from a line plot to solve problems involving range, average, and median? Use your observations to plan further instruction and review. (**1.** Check students' line plots. **2.** 6 3/4; **3.** 5; **4.** 5 3/4)

Model the Skill

◆ Hand out the Day 1 activity page.

◆ **Ask:** *What do you know about graphs? Why do we use graphs?* Record students' responses on the board.

◆ **Say:** *Today we are going to look at a graph called a line plot.* Have students look at the line plot and discuss the answers to problems 1 and 2. Help students understand that the scale is a number line and that each X records the value of one data point. The stack of Xs shows the frequency.

◆ **Ask:** *What do the acorns weigh? Where do you see that information?* (1, 1 1/2, 2, and 3 ounces; on the scale at the bottom of the graph)

◆ Help students complete the activity page. Point out that the number (or numbers) that occurs most often in a data set is called the mode. Students should count the number of Xs to determine how many acorns are in the data set. (**3.** 5, 2 ounces; **4.** 15)

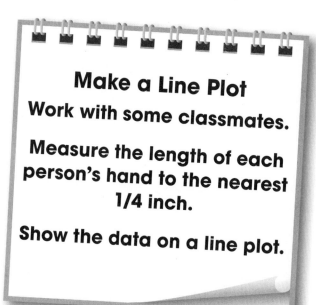

Make a Line Plot

Work with some classmates.

Measure the length of each person's hand to the nearest 1/4 inch.

Show the data on a line plot.

Use Measurement Data

Use the graph to answer the questions.

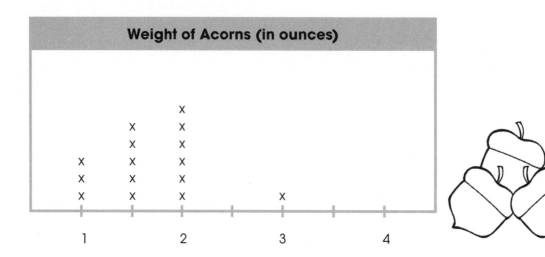

1 What information does the graph show?

_____

2 Why do you think this type of graph is called a line plot?

_____

3 How many acorns weigh $1\frac{1}{2}$ ounces? _____

What is the weight that occurred most often? _____

4 How many acorns were weighed? _____

☆ **Tell how you got your answer.**

Name _____

Use Measurement Data

A gardener sorts daffodil bulbs by size.
He can sell bigger bulbs for more money.

Use the graph to answer the questions.

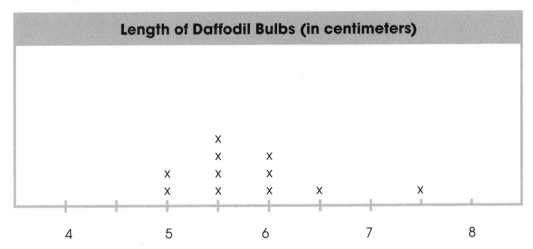

Length of Daffodil Bulbs (in centimeters)

1 What does the line plot show?

_____

2 What is the greatest value in this set of data? _____

What is the least value? _____

3 What is the difference between the greatest

value and least value? _____

4 What is the middle value (median) in this set of data? _____

⭐ **Tell how you found the median.**

Name _____

Use Measurement Data

A science experiment calls for test tubes to be filled with water in the amounts shown.

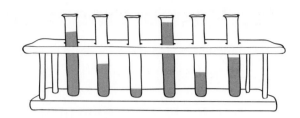

Use the graph to answer the questions.

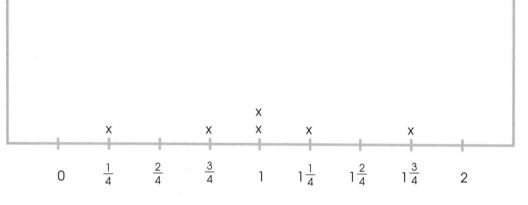

Experiment 1—Amount of Water (in fluid ounces)

0    $\frac{1}{4}$ $\frac{2}{4}$ $\frac{3}{4}$ 1 $1\frac{1}{4}$ $1\frac{2}{4}$ $1\frac{3}{4}$ 2

1 What does the line plot show?

_____

2 How many test tubes have water in them? _____

3 What is the difference between the least amount of water and the greatest amount of water?

_____

4 What if the water in the test tubes was redistributed so that each tube had the same amount? How much water would each tube have?

_____ fl oz

☆ **Tell how you solved the problem.**

Name _____

Use Measurement Data

Mrs. Barnes goes on a diet. She records how much weight she loses each week.

Pounds	Weeks
$\frac{1}{4}$	I
$\frac{1}{2}$	I I I
$\frac{3}{4}$	I I
$1\frac{1}{2}$	I I
$2\frac{3}{4}$	I

Complete the line plot below with the data in the table. Then answer the questions.

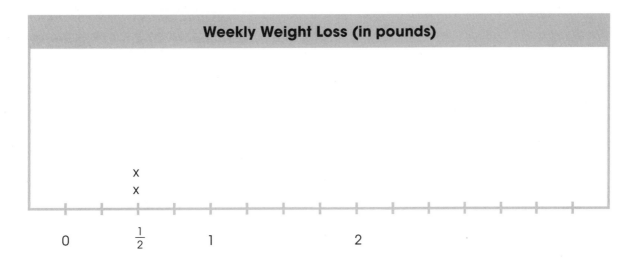

Weekly Weight Loss (in pounds)

```
        x
        x
 ┼──┼──┼──┼──┼──┼──┼──┼──┼──┼──┼──┼──┼
 0    1/2    1         2
```

1 How many weeks was Mrs. Barnes on the diet? _____

_____

2 What was the most frequent amount of weight lost? _____

_____

3 What was Mrs. Barnes's average weight loss? _____

_____

☆ **Tell another question the line plot could be used to answer.**

Assessment

One week last winter, it snowed almost every day.

Snowfall

Inches	Days
$1\frac{1}{4}$	l
2	l
$5\frac{3}{4}$	l
8	l l

① **Use the data in the table to complete the line plot.**

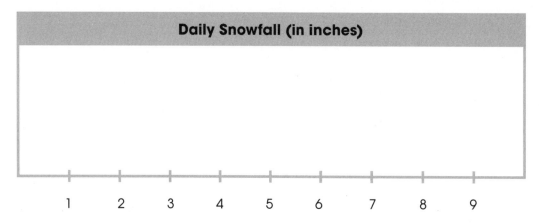

Daily Snowfall (in inches)

1 2 3 4 5 6 7 8 9

Use the line plot to answer the questions.

② What is the difference from the least amount of snow to the greatest amount?

_____ inches

③ What is the average amount of snow that fell each day?

_____ inches

④ What is the median snowfall?

_____ inches

☆ **Tell how you found the median and what it means.**

Overview   Understand Volume

Directions and Sample Answers for Activity Pages

Day 1	See "Model the Skill" below.
Day 2	Read the directions aloud. Have students solve the problems by using cm cubes to model the art. Have them draw the missing cubes on the art and write the volume. (**1.** 8; **2.** 18; **3.** 12)
Day 3	Discuss how to find volume by counting the number of cubic units in one layer and then adding layers. Students may see that they can multiply by the number of layers, but they should understand the additive nature of volume. (**1.** 9, 3, 9 + 9 + 9 = 27 cubic units; **2.** 12, 2, 12 + 12 = 24 cubic units; **3.** 6, 4, 24 cubic units)
Day 4	Read the directions aloud. You may also wish to read the word problems aloud. Direct students to use the art to find volume. Students may also use cm cubes to help them. (**1.** 64; **2.** 18; **3.** 15, 4; **4.** B)
Day 5	Read the directions aloud. Students may need to use centimeter cubes to help them. Observe as students complete the page. Do students demonstrate an understanding of volume and how to find volume by counting cubic units? Use your observations to plan further instruction and review. (**1.** 8 cubic units; **2.** 5 cubic cm; **3.** 12, 2, 24 cubic units; **4.** 40)

Model the Skill

◆ Hand out the Day 1 activity page and twelve centimeter cubes to each student.

◆ **Say:** *Today we are going measure volume. All solid shapes have volume. Who can tell me what volume is?* Record and discuss students' responses. Help students understand that a solid figure can be "packed" with cubic units, and that volume is the number of the cubic units that fill the figure without gaps or overlaps.

◆ **Say:** *Look at the activity page and at the centimeter cubes I gave you. How do you describe a cubic unit?* (Possible response: Each edge measures 1 unit, like 1 cm.)

◆ Help students complete the activity page. Have students place cm cubes on top of the art and count cubic units to find the volume of the box. (**1.** 9; **2.** 10; **3.** 12)

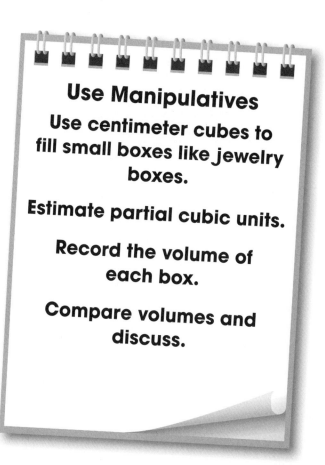

Use Manipulatives

Use centimeter cubes to fill small boxes like jewelry boxes.

Estimate partial cubic units.

Record the volume of each box.

Compare volumes and discuss.

Understand Volume

Count the cubic units to find the volume.

Unit Cube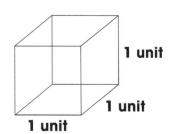

1 unit
1 unit
1 unit

Aera = 9
permeater = 12

3
HwL
3 3
3 3
3

① The volume is ___6___ cubic units.

Aera = 10
per mteater = 14

HwL
1 6 5
2
2

② The volume is ___16___ cubic units.

③ The volume is _____ cubic units.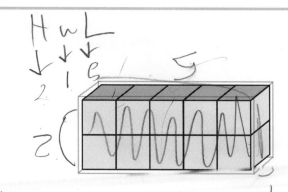

HwL
3 4

aera = 14
perimtrj 4
volume = 24

8 6

Name _____

Understand Volume

Use centimeter cubes. Draw to fill each box. Write the volume.

1 Cubic Centimeter

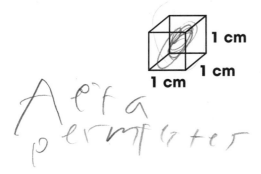

1   The volume is _____ cubic cm.

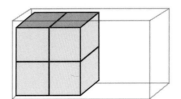

---

2   The volume is _____ cubic cm.

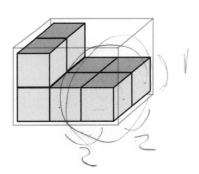

---

3   The volume is _____ cubic cm.

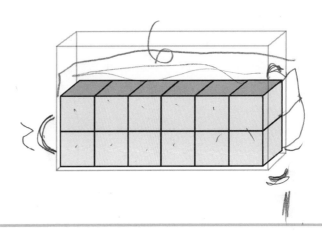

⭐ **Tell how you found the volume.**

Understand Volume

Find the volume.

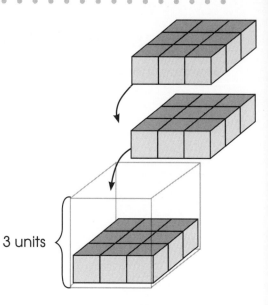

1 Number of cubic units in one layer: _____

Number of layers: _____

Volume: _____ + _____ + _____ = _____

3 units

2 Number of cubic units in one layer: _____

Number of layers: _____

Volume: _____ + _____ = _____

2 units

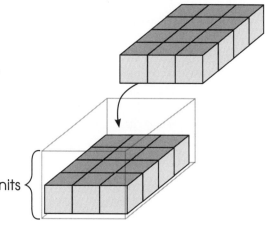

3 Number of cubic units in one layer: _____

Number of layers: _____

Volume: _____

4 units

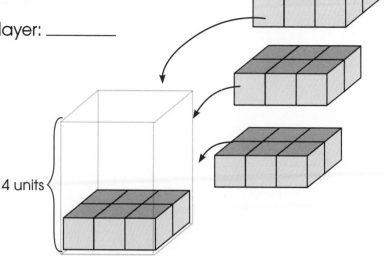

☆ **Tell how you solved the problem.**

      Unit 23 • Mathematics Intervention Activities Grade 5 • © 2014 Newmark Learning, LLC

Understand Volume

Solve each problem. Show your work.

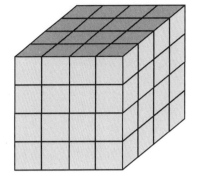

① Stacy wants to mail this box.
What is the volume of the box?

_____ cubic units

② Six cubic units fit in one layer of a box. The box
holds three layers. What is the volume of the box?

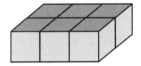

_____ cubic units

③ A little boy has blocks that are cubes. The blocks
fit in the wagon shown. What is the volume of the
wagon? How many blocks are missing?

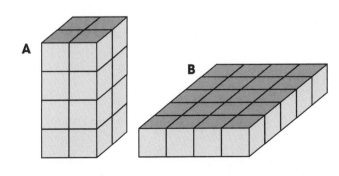

_____ cubic units   _____ blocks missing

④ Which rectangular prism has the
greater volume?

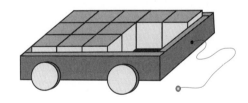

A

B

_____

⭐ **Tell how you solved the problem.**

Assessment

Solve each problem. Show your work.

1 What is the volume of this rectangular prism in cubic units?

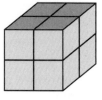

The volume is _____

---

2 What is the volume of this box in cubic centimeters?

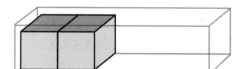

The volume is _____

---

3 Volume of one layer: _____

Number of layers: _____

Volume of box: _____

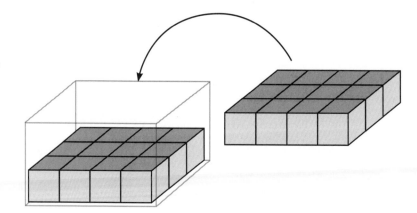

---

4 Eight cubic units fit in one layer of a box.
The box holds 5 layers. What is the volume of the box?

_____ cubic units

☆ **Tell how you solved the problem.**

Overview   Find Volume

Directions and Sample Answers for Activity Pages

Day 1	See "Model the Skill" below.
Day 2	Tell students that a formula is an equation that shows a mathematical relationship. We use that relationship to solve problems. Remind students that length, width, and height are measured in standard units of length. Area is measured in square units (l x w) and volume is measured in cubic units (l x w x h). Help students apply the formulas and complete the page. (**1.** 12 cm, 5 cm, 2 cm, 60 sq cm, 120 cu cm; **2.** 5 ft, 2 ft, 6 ft, 10 sq ft, 60 cu ft; **3.** 7 m, 3 m, 4 m, 21 sq m, 84 cu m)
Day 3	Read the directions aloud. Tell students that they can use the formula for volume to find missing dimensions by using the relationship between multiplication and division. Discuss how to solve problem 1. Help students complete the page. (**1.** 4, 40, 40, 2 cm; **2.** 7, 1, 7, 7, 4 cm; **3.** 3, 5, 15, 180 ÷ 15, 12 cm; **4.** 320 = 8 x 4 x h, 10 cm)
Day 4	Read the directions aloud. You may also wish to read the word problems aloud. Have students write the formula for volume and substitute values to solve problems. (**1.** 960; **2.** 720; **3.** 24; **4.** 10)
Day 5	Read the directions aloud. Observe as students complete the page. Can students use a formula to find the volume of a rectangular prism? Can they manipulate the formula to find a missing dimension? Use your observations to plan further instruction and review. (**1.** 8, 3, 6, 24 sq cm, 144 cu cm; **2.** 5, 5, 25, 125 ÷ 25, 5 cm; **3.** 4 cu ft; **4.** 5 cm)

Model the Skill

◆ Hand out the Day 1 activity page and fifty centimeter cubes per group.

◆ **Say:** *Today we are going to find the volume of rectangular prisms by using a formula.* Have students look at problem 1 and point to the rectangular prism, the height, and the base.

◆ **Ask:** *If we use centimeter cubes, how many cubes form the bottom layer of this prism?* (9) Tell students that the bottom layer is called the base. *If I want to find the area of the base, what should I do?* (multiply length times width) Remind students that area tells the number of square units and that it is not until they multiply by height (the third dimension) that they find cubic units of volume.

Use Manipulatives

Use a ruler. Measure length, width, and height to the nearest centimeter or inch of cereal boxes, shoe boxes, etc.

Find the volume of each box.

◆ Help students complete the activity page. Allow students to use cm cubes to model the problems, proving that the area of the base times the height yields the same answer as counting cubes and layers. (**1.** 9 sq cm, 9 x 3 = 27 cu cm; **2.** 4 sq m, 4 x 6 = 24 cu m; **3.** 24 sq ft, 24 x 2 = 48 cu ft)

Find Volume

Find the volume of each rectangular prism.

1

Area of the base: _____ sq cm

Height: 3 cm

Volume: _____ x _____ = _____

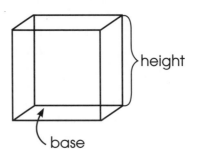

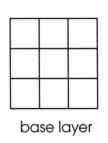

base layer

2

Area of the base: _____ sq m

Height: _____

Volume: _____ x _____ = _____

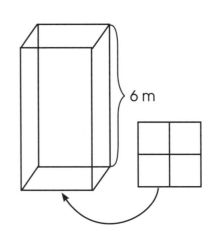

3

Area of the base: _____ sq ft

Height: _____

Volume: _____ x _____ = _____

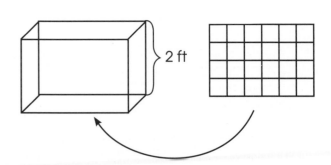

 Tell how you can use area to find volume.

Find Volume

Use a formula to find volume. Show your work.

Formulas for Volume of a Rectangular Prism	
Volume = base (area of) x height	$V = b \times h$
Volume = length x width x height	$V = l \times w \times h$

---

1 length _____ width _____ height _____

area of base _____

Volume _____

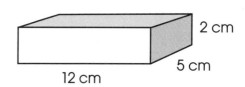

2 cm
5 cm
12 cm

---

2 length _____ width _____ height _____

area of base _____

Volume _____

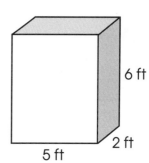

6 ft
2 ft
5 ft

---

3 length _____ width _____ height _____

area of base _____

Volume _____

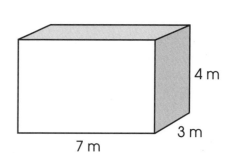

4 m
3 m
7 m

 Tell how you found the volume.

Find Volume

Find the missing dimension. Use the formula *V = l x w x h*.

1 $V = l \times w \times h$

Volume: 80 cu cm

$80 = 10 \times \underline{\hspace{2cm}} \times h$

$80 = \underline{\hspace{2cm}} \times h$

$h = 80 \div \underline{\hspace{2cm}}$

$h = \underline{\hspace{2cm}}$

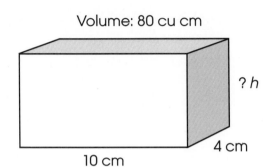

? h

10 cm   4 cm

---

2 $V = l \times w \times h$

$28 = \underline{\hspace{2cm}} \times w \times \underline{\hspace{2cm}}$

$28 = \underline{\hspace{2cm}} \times w$

$w = 28 \div \underline{\hspace{2cm}}$

$w = \underline{\hspace{2cm}}$

Volume: 28 cu cm

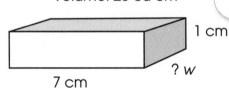

1 cm

7 cm   ? w

Remember: You can multiply in any order.

---

3 $V = l \times w \times h$

$180 = l \times \underline{\hspace{2cm}} \times \underline{\hspace{2cm}}$

$180 = l \times \underline{\hspace{2cm}}$

$l = \underline{\hspace{2cm}} \div \underline{\hspace{2cm}}$

$l = \underline{\hspace{2cm}}$

Volume: 180 cu cm

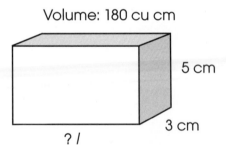

5 cm

3 cm

? l

---

4 $V = l \times w \times h$

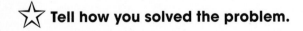
$\underline{\hspace{2cm}} = \underline{\hspace{2cm}} \times \underline{\hspace{2cm}} \times \underline{\hspace{2cm}}$

$h = \underline{\hspace{2cm}}$

Volume: 320 cu cm

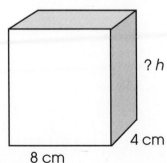

? h

4 cm

8 cm

☆ **Tell how you solved the problem.**

Find Volume

Solve each problem. Show your work.

① The height of a room is 10 feet.
The area of the floor is 96 square feet.
What is the volume of the room?

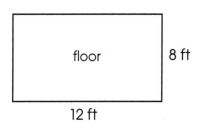

floor   8 ft

12 ft

_____ cubic feet

② A fish tank measures 10 in. by 8 in. by 9 in.
What is the volume of the fish tank?

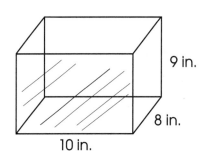

9 in.

8 in.

10 in.

_____ cubic inches

③ A rectangular prism measures 4 meters long
and 3 meters wide. Its height is 2 meters.
What is the volume of the prism?

_____ cubic meters

④ The volume of a box is 360 cubic centimeters.
Its length and width are each 6 centimeters.
What is the height of the box?

_____ cm

☆ **Tell how you solved the problem.**

Assessment

Solve each problem. Show your work.

1

length _____ width _____ height _____

area of base _____

Volume _____

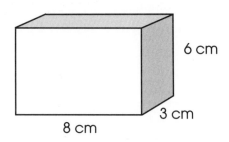

6 cm

3 cm

8 cm

2

$V = l \times w \times h$

$125 = l \times$ _____ $\times$ _____

$125 = l \times$ _____

$l =$ _____ $\div$ _____

$l =$ _____

Volume: 125 cu cm

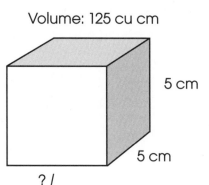

5 cm

5 cm

? l

---

3 An ice chest measures 2 feet long and 1 foot wide. Its height is 2 feet. What is the volume of the ice chest?

_____ cubic feet

---

4 The volume of a rectangular prism is 90 cubic centimeters. The height is 2 cm and the length is 9 cm. What is the width?

_____ cm

 Tell how you know your answer is correct.

Overview   Graph Points on the Coordinate Plane

Directions and Sample Answers for Activity Pages

Day 1	See "Model the Skill" below.
Day 2	Remind students to write the number for the *x*-axis first in an ordered pair. If time allows, have students put other points on the grid and write ordered pairs. (**1.** (1,1); **2.** (3,11); **3.** (7,9); **4.** (3,6); **5.** (8,2))
Day 3	Read the directions aloud. Help students complete the page. Students should have a straight line when they connect the points. Show them how to find another related coordinate by extending the line. (Check students' graphs.)
Day 4	Read the directions aloud. You may also wish to read the word problems aloud. Problem 2 requires students to use information from text to plot and extend a line. There is more than one way to solve the problem. (Check students' graphs. **1.** 4, 2, 12, 3; **2.** 3, 6, 9, 12, 30)
Day 5	Read the directions aloud. Observe as students complete the page. Can students locate points on a coordinate grid? Can they write ordered pairs and plot them on a coordinate grid? Use your observations to plan further instruction and review. (**1.** (3, 9); **2.** (12, 4); **3–4.** Check students' graphs.)

Model the Skill

◆ Hand out the Day 1 activity page.

◆ **Ask:** *What do you know about a coordinate plane? What are coordinates? How are they used?* Record students' responses. Tell students that the plane is two-dimensional space and coordinates are the numbers that let us locate points in that space, like coordinates on a map or GPS.

◆ **Say:** *We need to know a lot of special words to talk about the coordinate system.* Have students look at the page and point to the grid, the lines or axes that form the grid, the horizontal *x*-axis, the vertical *y*-axis, and the origin where the axes meet.

◆ **Say:** *We use ordered pairs to locate points. Ordered pairs are coordinates. Look at problem 1. The first number (x) tells how far to move along the x-axis. The second number in the ordered pair (y) tells how far to move along the y-axis.*

◆ Help students complete the activity page, drawing lines across and up the grid to locate points. Emphasize that order is important. (**1.** home; **2.** library; **3.** soccer field; **4.** school)

Play Battleship

Two players each have a coordinate grid.

Players mark ships on the grid without allowing the other player to see.

Players take turns giving coordinates to locate the other player's ships.

Graph Points on the Coordinate Plane

Start at the origin and draw how to move to each point.
Write what is located at each point.

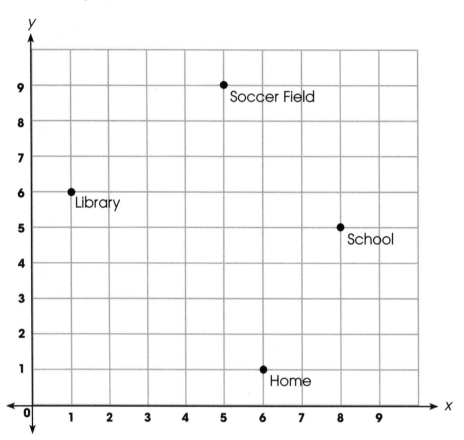

1

x	y
6	1

_____

2

x	y
1	6

_____

3

x	y
5	9

_____

4

x	y
8	5

_____

⭐ **Tell how you locate points on a coordinate grid.**

Graph Points on the Coordinate Plane

Write the ordered pair for each point.

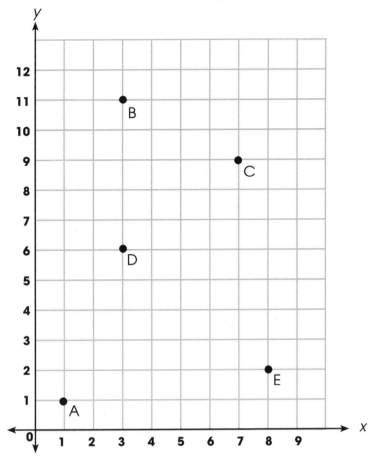

1. Point A: (_____,_____)

2. Point B: (_____,_____)

3. Point C: (_____,_____)

4. Point D: (_____,_____)

5. Point E: (_____,_____)

⭐ **Tell how you write an ordered pair.**

Graph Points on the Coordinate Plane

Graph each ordered pair.

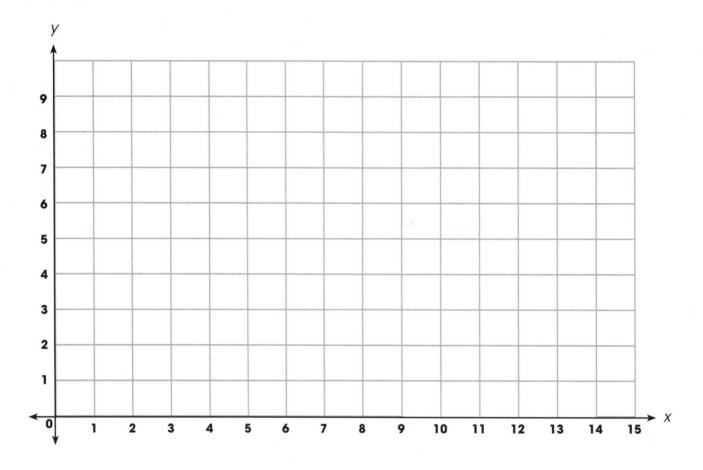

	x	y
1	3	1
2	6	2
3	9	3
4	12	4

☆ **Connect the points and tell what you notice.**

Graph Points on the Coordinate Plane

Use the graph to solve the problem.

1 Complete the table to show how many quarts
   are in 1 or more gallons. Use the graph to help you.

qt	gal
x	y
	1
8	

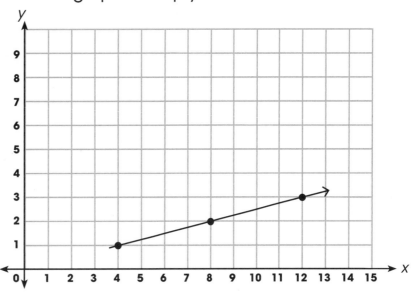

Complete the table and plot the points to help you solve the problem.

2 In 1 minute, a machine can make 3 erasers.
   In 2 minutes, it can make 6 erasers.
   In 3 minutes, it can make 9 erasers.
   How many erasers can the machine
   make in 10 minutes?

input	output
x	y
1	
2	
3	
4	

_____ erasers in 10 minutes

⭐ **Tell how you solved the problem.**

Assessment

Use the coordinate grid for each problem.

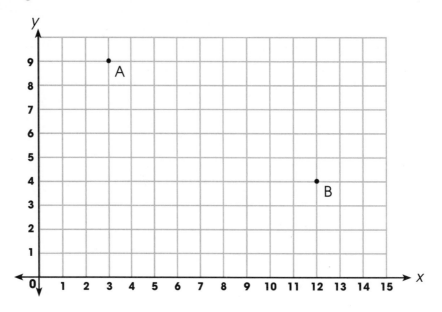

1. Write the ordered pair for point A. _____

2. Write the ordered pair for point B. _____

3. Graph point C on the coordinate grid.
Use the ordered pair in the table.

x	y
7	1

4. Graph point D on the coordinate grid. Use the ordered pair in the table.

x	y
10	9

☆ **Tell how you use an ordered pair to graph a point.**

Overview Classify Polygons

Directions and Sample Answers for Activity Pages

Day 1	See "Model the Skill" below.
Day 2	Read the directions aloud. Have students sketch quadrilaterals that have the properties given. Help students complete the page. You may wish to have students give the names of the quadrilaterals they draw. (**1.** any two quadrilaterals; **2.** square and rhombus; **3.** trapezoid)
Day 3	Tell students that today they will draw different kinds of parallelograms. Define parallelogram as a quadrilateral with two pairs of congruent and parallel sides. Draw different shapes on the board and have students identify the parallelogram. Read the directions aloud and help students complete the page. (**1.** any rectangle; **2.** square; **3.** rhombus)
Day 4	Read the directions aloud. Help students understand the oval graphic, with Rectangle being the narrowest category and Polygon the broadest. Figures that are rectangles are also parallelograms, quadrilaterals, and polygons. Have students use properties of each polygon to classify it in the narrowest category possible. (narrowest category given: **1.** polygon; **2.** rectangle; **3.** parallelogram; **4.** quadrilateral)
Day 5	Read the directions aloud. Observe as students complete the page. Can students sketch a quadrilateral to match a given property? Can they use properties to classify polygons? Note: The trapezoid in problem 4 means the group cannot be classified as parallelograms. Use your observations to plan further instruction and review. (**1.** any quadrilateral with two or no parallel sides; **2.** square; **3.** rectangles; **4.** quadrilaterals)

Model the Skill

◆ Hand out the Day 1 activity page.

◆ **Say:** *We are going to use properties of polygons over the next few days to classify two-dimensional figures.* Remind students that a polygon is a closed, flat shape with sides that are line segments. Have students list the names of as many polygons as they can. Then have them look at the activity page.

◆ **Ask:** *What are some properties of polygons?* (number of sides and angles, congruent sides, parallel sides, right angles)

◆ Read the directions aloud. Help students complete the activity page. Discuss each match to help students understand the vocabulary. (Check students' work.)

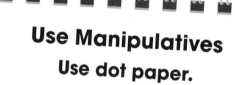

Use Manipulatives

Use dot paper.

Draw a quadrilateral. Do not let your partner see the picture. Describe its sides and angles.

Your partner draws the figure from your description.

Classify Polygons

Match. Draw a line from one figure to each description.

1. angle

2. congruent

3. parallel

4. parallelogram

5. quadrilateral

6. rectangle

7. right angle

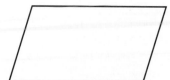

⭐ **Tell what *parallel* means.**

Classify Polygons

Use the dot paper to draw the figures.

① Draw two different polygons that have four sides and four angles.

. . . .
. . . .
. . . .
. . . .
. . . .
. . . .
. . . .
. . . .
. . . .
. . . .

② Draw two different quadrilaterals that have two pairs of congruent and parallel sides.

. . . .
. . . .
. . . .
. . . .
. . . .
. . . .
. . . .
. . . .
. . . .

③ Draw a quadrilateral with exactly one pair of parallel sides.

. . . .
. . . .
. . . .
. . . .
. . . .
. . . .
. . . .
. . . .
. . . .

☆ **Tell how a rectangle is different from the quadrilateral you drew.**

Classify Polygons

Draw each figure.

1 a parallelogram with four right angles

2 a parallelogram with four
   congruent sides and four right angles

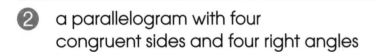

3 a parallelogram with four
   congruent sides and two pairs
   of congruent angles

⭐ **Tell what are the properties of a parallelogram.**

Classify Polygons

Classify each polygon into categories. Write as many categories as apply.

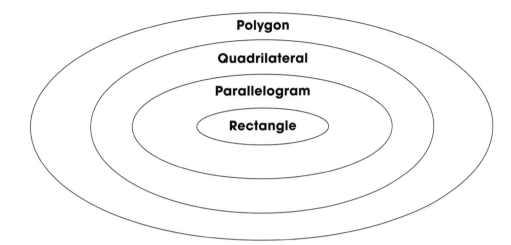

1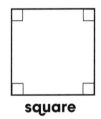

pentagon

_____

2

square

_____

3

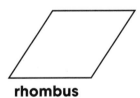

rhombus

_____

4

trapezoid

_____

⭐ **Tell why a rectangle is also a parallelogram.**

Assessment

Draw each figure.

1 a quadrilateral that is not a parallelogram

2 a quadrilateral that has congruent sides and right angles

Classify each group of figures. Write "quadrilaterals," "parallelograms," or "rectangles."

3
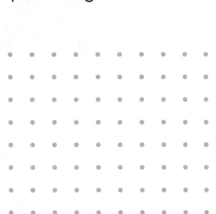

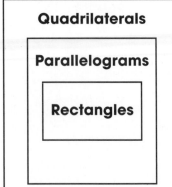

_____

4
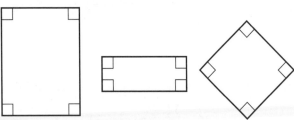

_____

 Tell why you classified the group the way you did.